Hambleton Hall

—

MORE POETRY PLEASE!

MORE P○ETRY PLEASE!

A FURTHER SELECTION
of POPULAR P○EMS
from the RADIO 4 SERIES

Edited by SUSAN ROBERTS

BBC BOOKS

I would like to thank Linda Sommer, a name familiar to regular
correspondents for her help and prolific letter writing, Julian
Wilkinson, a valuable new addition to the team, my mother, for her
help and photocopying, and especially, Simon Rae who, as well as
being the regular presenter of *Poetry Please!*, introduces the selection of
poems in this book.

My thanks also go to the poets who have taken part in the
programme over the past months, and to all our poetry readers whose
versatile interpretations bring requested poems to life, week after
week.

Published by BBC Books,
a division of BBC Enterprises Limited,
Woodlands, 80 Wood Lane
London W12 0TT

First published 1992

ISBN 0 563 36716 4

Set in 11/13 Garamond Roman by Ace Filmsetting Ltd, Frome
Printed and bound in Great Britain by Redwood Press Ltd, Melksham
Jacket printed by Belmont Press Ltd, Northampton

CONTENTS

7

FOREWORD
by Simon Rae

I have now been presenting *Poetry Please!* for three years. It has been a great privilege. Radio is an exciting medium to work in, whatever the programme, but *Poetry Please!* is special. I'm sure all programmes have loyal and devoted listeners, but few can boast as close a relationship as we enjoy with our audience.

Week after week the letters flood in, bearing requests not only for well- or little-known poems and poets, but also memories, opinions, inquiries and, to be fair, criticism too, sometimes. But who would want to produce a programme for an uncritical audience? In recent years, we have taken the programme out of the studio for more and more live recordings, which has given the opportunity to meet some of the many hundreds of thousands who tune in each week. *Poetry Please!* is, more than almost any other programme on the network, a listeners' programme.

And this, the second *Poetry Please!* anthology edited by the programme producer, Susan Roberts, is very much a listeners' collection of poems. Once again, the computer files have been consulted, the popularity stakes assessed, and another wholly heterogeneous selection drawn together to delight, remind, intrigue and enthuse the reader.

What can be said about it? It's the same mixture as before – an assortment of poems by poets so famous they have streets and tower blocks named after them, to little-known poets, forgotten by all except the listeners for whom they mean so many special things.

Reading through the book, I am struck forcibly again by the extraordinary range of subject matter in English poetry. In the 'A's alone we have an adolescent with a rebellious hairstyle, Maya Angelou's spirited hymn to freedom, 'Still I Rise', Matthew Arnold's rather less up-beat anticipation of old age, Auden's wonderfully compelling ballad, 'As I Walked Out One Evening', a poem that still makes the hair stir on the back of my neck every time I read it. And don't let's forget that most redoubtable of all English poets, Anon, the equivalent for poetry, I sometimes think, of Edward Thomas's timeless countryman, Lob. In this selection, Anon is responsible for the medieval religious vision, 'The Dream of the Rood', the well-loved song, 'I Sing of a Maiden' and a Second-World-War soldier's moving reverie of the battlefield.

And that's just (some of) the 'A's. For the rest, there are enough of my favourites to ensure the book an honoured place by my bedside: Browning's 'How They Brought the Good News from Ghent to Aix', Lewis Carroll's 'Father William', John Clare's 'I Am', John Davidson's rhythmical *tour de force*, 'A Runnable Stag', and poems by Philip Larkin, Walter de la Mare, Hopkins, MacNeice and Alfred, Lord Tennyson . . .

But there are also poems by contemporary poets. Some have come on the programme – James Fenton for instance, represented here by 'Song', one of his most powerful short poems. U. A. Fanthorpe, whose 'Not My Best Side', about the famous Uccello painting of St George and the Dragon, remains a great favourite, Andrew Motion and Peter Porter all have poems here, proving, if proof were needed, that there is a continuity between the established canon of English poetry and modern work. Every poet in this anthology was a new and unknown poet once. Each new generation has to struggle to assert itself. What seems strange and outlandish at first, later establishes itself as the prevailing orthodoxy – only to be challenged by the next generation in its turn.

Many, though by no means all, the poems here are classics. But whatever their status in the critical hierarchy, what matters is that some among our listeners have expressed a strong affection for them. Often letters requesting a particular poem go on to say that it is 'too good not to be shared'. And it's that spirit of generous enthusiasm that lies at the root of this *More Poetry Please!* anthology.

I hope you'll enjoy it. I'm sure you will.

Fleur Adcock 1934–

FOR HEIDI WITH BLUE HAIR

When you dyed your hair blue
(or, at least, ultramarine
for the clipped sides, with a crest
of jet-black spikes on top)
you were sent home from school

because, as the headmistress put it,
although dyed hair was not
specifically forbidden, yours
was, apart from anything else,
not done in the school colours.

Tears in the kitchen, telephone-calls
to school from your freedom-loving father:
'She's not a punk in her behaviour;
it's just a style.' (You wiped your eyes,
also not in a school colour.)

'She discussed it with me first –
we checked the rules.' 'And anyway, Dad,
it cost twenty-five dollars.
Tell them it won't wash out –
not even if I wanted to try.'

It would have been unfair to mention
your mother's death, but that
shimmered behind the arguments.
The school had nothing else against you;
the teachers twittered and gave in.

Next day your black friend had hers done
in grey, white and flaxen yellow –
the school colours precisely:
an act of solidarity, a witty
tease. The battle was already won.

FOUR DUCKS ON A POND

Four ducks on a pond,
A grass-bank beyond,
A blue sky of spring,
White clouds on the wing;
What a little thing
To remember for years –
To remember with tears!

Maya Angelou 1928–

STILL I RISE

You may write me down in history
With your bitter, twisted lies,
You may trod me in the very dirt
But still, like dust, I'll rise.

Does my sassiness upset you?
Why are you beset with gloom?
'Cause I walk like I've got oil wells
Pumping in my living room.

Just like moons and like suns,
With the certainty of tides,
Just like hopes springing high,
Still I'll rise.

Did you want to see me broken?
Bowed head and lowered eyes?
Shoulders falling down like teardrops,
Weakened by my soulful cries.

Does my haughtiness offend you?
Don't you take it awful hard
'Cause I laugh like I've got gold mines
Diggin' in my own back yard.

You may shoot me with your words,
You may cut me with your eyes,
You may kill me with your hatefulness,
But still, like air, I'll rise.

Does my sexiness upset you?
Does it come as a surprise
That I dance like I've got diamonds
At the meeting of my thighs?

Out of the huts of history's shame
I rise
Up from a past that's rooted in pain
I rise
I'm a black ocean, leaping and wide,
Welling and swelling I bear in the tide.

Leaving behind nights of terror and fear
I rise
Into a daybreak that's wondrously clear
I rise
Bringing the gifts that my ancestors gave,
I am the dream and the hope of the slave.
I rise
I rise
I rise.

A SOLDIER – HIS PRAYER

(This anonymous poem was blown by the wind into a slit trench
at El Agheila during a heavy bombardment.)

Stay with me, God. The night is dark,
The night is cold: my little spark
Of courage dies. The night is long;
Be with me, God, and make me strong.

I love a game, I love a fight.
I hate the dark; I love the light.
I love my child; I love my wife.
I am no coward. I love Life,

Life with its change of mood and shade.
I want to live. I'm not afraid,
But me and mine are hard to part;
Oh, unknown God, lift up my heart.

You stilled the waters at Dunkirk
And saved Your Servants. All your work
Is wonderful, dear God. You strode
Before us down that dreadful road.

We were alone, and hope had fled;
We loved our country and our dead,
And could not shame them; so we stayed
The course, and were not much afraid.

Dear God, that nightmare road! And then
That sea! We got there – we were men.
My eyes were blind, my feet were torn,
My soul sang like a bird at dawn!

I knew that death is but a door.
I knew what we were fighting for:
Peace for the kids, our brothers freed,
A kinder world, a cleaner breed.

I'm but the son my mother bore,
A simple man, and nothing more.
But – God of strength and gentleness
Be pleased to make me nothing less.

Help me, O God, when Death is near
To mock the haggard face of fear,
That when I fall – if fall I must –
My soul may triumph in the Dust.

Anon composed between the Seventh and Tenth Century
(Translated by Michael Alexander)

HWÆT! A DREAM CAME TO ME AT DEEP MIDNIGHT

From 'The Dream of the Rood'

Hwaet!
A dream came to me
    at deep midnight
when humankind
    kept their beds
– the dream of dreams!
    I shall declare it.

It seemed I saw the Tree itself
borne on the air, light wound about it,
– a beam of brightest wood, a beacon clad
in overlapping gold, glancing gems
fair at its foot, and five stones
set in a crux flashed from the crosstree . . . .

. . . Yet lying there a long while
I beheld, sorrowing, the Healer's Tree
till it seemed that I heard how it broke silence,
best of wood, and began to speak:

'Over that long remove my mind ranges
back to the holt where I was hewn down;
from my own stem I was struck away,
   dragged off by strong enemies,
wrought into a roadside scaffold,
   They made me a hoist for wrongdoers.

The soldiers on their shoulders bore me,
   until on a hill-top they set me up;
many enemies made me fast there.
   Then I saw, marching toward me,

17

mankind's brave King;
     He came to climb upon me.

I dared not break or bend aside
against God's will, though the ground itself
shook at my feet. Fast I stood,
who falling could have felled them all.

Almighty God ungirded Him,
     eager to mount the gallows,
unafraid in the sight of many:
     He would set free mankind.
I shook when His arms embraced me
     but I durst not bow to ground,
stoop to Earth's surface.
     Stand fast I must.

I was reared up, a rood.
     I raised the great King,
liege lord of the heavens,
     dared not lean from the true.
They drove me through with dark nails:
     on me are the deep wounds manifest,
wide-mouthed hate dents.
          I durst not harm any of them.
How they mocked at us both!
          I was all moist with blood
sprung from the Man's side
          after He sent forth His soul.

Wry wierds a-many I underwent
up on that hill-top; saw the Lord of Hosts
stretched out stark. Darkness shrouded
the King's corse. Clouds wrapped
its clear shining. A shade went out
wan under cloud-pall. All creation wept,
keened the King's death. Christ was on the Cross . . . .'

I SING OF A MAIDEN

I sing of a maiden
    That is makéless:
King of all kingés
    To her son she ches.

He came all so stillé
    There his mother was
As dew in Aprílle
    That falleth on the grass.

He came all so stillé
    To his mother's bower
As dew in Aprílle
    That falleth on the flower.

He came all so stillé
    There his mother lay
As dew in Aprílle
    That falleth on the spray.

Mother and maiden
    Was never none but she;
Well may such a lady
    Goddés mother be.

GROWING OLD

What is it to grow old?
Is it to lose the glory of the form,
The lustre of the eye?
Is it for beauty to forgo her wreath?
– Yes, but not this alone.

Is it to feel our strength –
Not our bloom only, but our strength – decay?
Is it to feel each limb
Grow stiffer, every function less exact,
Each nerve more loosely strung?

Yes, this, and more; but not
Ah, 'tis not what in youth we dreamed 'twould be!
'Tis not to have our life
Mellowed and softened as with sunset-glow,
A golden day's decline.

'Tis not to see the world
As from a height, with rapt prophetic eyes,
And heart profoundly stirred;
And weep, and feel the fullness of the past,
The years that are no more.

It is to spend long days
And not once feel that we were ever young;
It is to add, immured
In the hot prison of the present, month
To month with weary pain.

It is to suffer this,
And feel but half, and feebly, what we feel.
Deep in our hidden heart
Festers the dull remembrance of a change,
But no emotion – none.

It is – last stage of all –
When we are frozen up within, and quite
The phantom of ourselves,
To hear the world applaud the hollow ghost
Which blamed the living man.

AS I WALKED OUT ONE EVENING

As I walked out one evening,
    Walking down Bristol Street,
The crowds upon the pavement
    Were fields of harvest wheat.

And down by the brimming river
    I heard a lover sing
Under an arch of the railway:
    'Love has no ending.

'I'll love you, dear, I'll love you
    Till China and Africa meet,
And the river jumps over the mountain
    And the salmon sing in the street,

'I'll love you till the ocean
    Is folded and hung up to dry
And the seven stars go squawking
    Like geese about the sky.

The years shall run like rabbits,
    For in my arms I hold
The Flower of the Ages,
    And the first love of the world.'

But all the clocks in the city
    Began to whirr and chime:
'O let not Time deceive you,
    You cannot conquer Time.

'In the burrows of the Nightmare
    Where Justice naked is,
Time watches from the shadow
    And coughs when you would kiss.

22

'In headaches and in worry
    Vaguely life leaks away,
And Time will have his fancy
    To-morrow or to-day.

'Into many a green valley
    Drifts the appalling snow;
Time breaks the threaded dances
    And the diver's brilliant bow.

'O plunge your hands in water,
    Plunge them in up to the wrist;
Stare, stare in the basin
    And wonder what you've missed.

'The glacier knocks in the cupboard,
    The desert sighs in the bed,
And the crack in the tea-cup opens
    A lane to the land of the dead.

'Where the beggars raffle the banknotes
    And the Giant is enchanting to Jack,
And the Lily-white Boy is a Roarer,
    And Jill goes down on her back.

'O look, look in the mirror,
    O look in your distress;
Life remains a blessing
    Although you cannot bless.

'O stand, stand at the window
    As the tears scald and start;
You shall love your crooked neighbour
    With your crooked heart.'

It was late, late in the evening,
    The lovers they were gone;
The clocks had ceased their chiming,
    And the deep river ran on.

THE YAK

As a friend to the children commend me the Yak.
  You will find it exactly the thing:
It will carry and fetch, you can ride on its back,
  Or lead it about with a string.

The Tartar who dwells on the plains of Thibet
  (A desolate region of snow)
Has for centuries made it a nursery pet,
  And surely the Tartar should know!

Then tell your papa where the Yak can be got,
  And if he is awfully rich
He will buy you the creature – or else he will *not*.
  (I cannot be positive which.)

Edward Berryman 1914–

COTSWOLD TILES

The finest roofs in all the land are made from Cotswold stone,
And the mason gives each tile a name like children of his
    own.
By length and breadth the tally runs, by width and depth and
    size,
And the mason knows them all by name, for he is very wise.

Long Day, Short Day, Moreday and Muffity,
Lye-byes and Bottomers, each a name receives:
Wivett, Beck, and Cussomes, Cutting, Third and Bachelor,
Smallest under roof-ridge, largest over eaves.

Each tile in its own special place is hung with loving care,
And they weather down the ages in the mellow Cotswold air:
Twenty-six in all there are – the family's not small,
I can but tell you one or two, I can't remember all.

Long Day, Short Day, Moreday and Muffity,
Lye-byes and Bottomers, each a name receives:
Wivett, Beck, and Cussomes, Cutting, Third and Bachelor,
Smallest under roof-ridge, largest over eaves.

A SUBALTERN'S LOVE-SONG

Miss J. Hunter Dunn, Miss J. Hunter Dunn,
Furnish'd and burnish'd by Aldershot sun,
What strenuous singles we played after tea,
We in the tournament – you against me!

Love-thirty, love-forty, oh! weakness of joy,
The speed of a swallow, the grace of a boy,
With carefullest carelessness, gaily you won,
I am weak from your loveliness, Joan Hunter Dunn.

Miss Joan Hunter Dunn, Miss Joan Hunter Dunn,
How mad I am, sad I am, glad that you won.
The warm-handled racket is back in its press,
But my shock-headed victor, she loves me no less.

Her father's euonymus shines as we walk,
And swing past the summer-house, buried in talk,
And cool the verandah that welcomes us in
To the six-o'clock news and a lime-juice and gin.

The scent of the conifers, sound of the bath,
The view from my bedroom of moss-dappled path,
As I struggle with double-end evening tie,
For we dance at the Golf Club, my victor and I.

On the floor of her bedroom lie blazer and shorts
And the cream-coloured walls are be-trophied with sports,
And westering, questioning settles the sun
On your low-leaded window, Miss Joan Hunter Dunn.

The Hillman is waiting, the light's in the hall,
The pictures of Egypt are bright on the wall,
My sweet, I am standing beside the oak stair
And there on the landing's the light on your hair.

By roads 'not adopted', by woodlanded ways,
She drove to the club in the late summer haze,
Into nine-o'clock Camberley, heavy with bells
And mushroomy, pine-woody, evergreen smells.

Miss Joan Hunter Dunn, Miss Joan Hunter Dunn,
I can hear from the car-park the dance has begun.
Oh! full Surrey twilight! importunate band!
Oh! strongly adorable tennis-girl's hand!

Around us are Rovers and Austins afar,
Above us, the intimate roof of the car,
And here on my right is the girl of my choice,
With the tilt of her nose and the chime of her voice,

And the scent of her wrap, and the words never said,
And the ominous, ominous dancing ahead.
We sat in the car park till twenty to one
And now I'm engaged to Miss Joan Hunter Dunn.

William Blake 1757–1827

THE TYGER

Tyger Tyger, burning bright,
In the forests of the night:
What immortal hand or eye,
Could frame thy fearful symmetry?

In what distant deeps or skies
Burnt the fire of thine eyes!
On what wings dare he aspire?
What the hand, dare seize the fire?

And what shoulder, & what art,
Could twist the sinews of thy heart?
And when thy heart began to beat,
What dread hand? & what dread feet?

What the hammer? what the chain,
In what furnace was thy brain?
What the anvil? what dread grasp,
Dare its deadly terrors clasp?

When the stars threw down their spears
And water'd heaven with their tears:
Did he smile his work to see?
Did he who made the Lamb make thee?

Tyger, Tyger burning bright,
In the forests of the night:
What immortal hand or eye,
Dare frame thy fearful symmetry?

Robert Bridges 1844–1930

I LOVE ALL BEAUTEOUS THINGS

I love all beauteous things,
    I seek and adore them;
God hath no better praise,
And man in his hasty days
    Is honoured for them.

I too will something make
    And joy in the making;
Altho' to-morrow it seem
Like the empty words of a dream
    Remembered on waking.

Emily Brontë 1818–48

THE OLD STOIC

Riches I hold in light esteem
And Love I laugh to scorn
And Lust of Fame was but a dream
That vanished with the morn –

And if I pray – the only prayer
That moves my lips for me
Is – 'Leave the heart that now I bear
And give me liberty.'

Yes, as my swift days near their goal
'Tis all that I implore –
In life and death, a chainless soul
With courage to endure!

Rupert Brooke 1887–1915

THE GREAT LOVER

I have been so great a lover: filled my days
So proudly with the splendour of Love's praise,
The pain, the calm, and the astonishment,
Desire illimitable, and still content,
And all dear names men use, to cheat despair,
For the perplexed and viewless streams that bear
Our hearts at random down the dark of life.
Now, ere the unthinking silence on that strife
Steals down, I would cheat drowsy Death so far,
My night shall be remembered for a star
That outshone all the suns of all men's days.
Shall I not crown them with immortal praise
Whom I have loved, who have given me, dared with me
High secrets, and in darkness knelt to see
The inenarrable godhead of delight?
Love is a flame: – we have beaconed the world's night.
A city: – and we have built it, these and I.
An emperor: – we have taught the world to die.
So, for their sakes I loved, ere I go hence,
And the high cause of Love's magnificence,
And to keep loyalties young, I'll write those names
Golden for ever, eagles, crying flames,
And set them as a banner, that men may know,
To dare the generations, burn, and blow
Out on the wind of Time, shining and streaming . . .

T. E. Brown 1830–97

MY GARDEN

A garden is a lovesome thing, God wot!
Rose plot,
Fringed pool,
Ferned grot –
The veriest school
Of peace; and yet the fool
Contends that God is not –
Not God! in gardens! when the eve is cool?
Nay, but I have a sign;
'Tis very sure God walks in mine.

Robert Browning 1812–89

HOW THEY BROUGHT THE GOOD NEWS FROM GHENT TO AIX
[16–]

I

I sprang to the stirrup, and Joris, and he;
I galloped, Dirck galloped, we galloped all three;
'Good speed!' cried the watch, as the gate-bolts undrew;
'Speed!' echoed the wall to us galloping through;
Behind shut the postern, the lights sank to rest,
And into the midnight we galloped abreast.

II

Not a word to each other; we kept the great pace
Neck by neck, stride by stride, never changing our place;
I turned in my saddle and made its girths tight,
Then shortened each stirrup, and set the pique right,
Rebuckled the cheek-strap, chained slacker the bit,
Nor galloped less steadily Roland a whit.

III

'Twas moonset at starting; but while we drew near
Lokeren, the cocks crew and twilight dawned clear;
At Boom, a great yellow star came out to see;
At Düffeld, 'twas morning as plain as could be;
And from Mecheln church-steeple we heard the half-chime,
So Joris broke silence with, 'Yet there is time!'

IV

At Aerschot, up leaped of a sudden the sun,
And against him the cattle stood black every one,
To stare thro' the mist at us galloping past,
And I saw my stout galloper Roland at last,
With resolute shoulders, each butting away
The haze, as some bluff river headland its spray.

V

And his low head and crest, just one sharp ear bent back
For my voice, and the other pricked out on his track;
And one eye's black intelligence, – ever that glance
O'er its white edge at me, his own master, askance!
And the thick heavy spume-flakes which aye and anon
His fierce lips shook upwards in galloping on.

VI

By Hasselt, Dirck groaned; and cried Joris, 'Stay spur!
Your Roos galloped bravely, the fault's not in her,
We'll remember at Aix' – for one heard the quick wheeze
Of her chest, saw the stretched neck and staggering knees,
And sunk tail, and horrible heave of the flank,
As down on her haunches she shuddered and sank.

VII

So we were left galloping, Joris and I,
Past Looz and past Tongres, no cloud in the sky;
The broad sun above laughed a pitiless laugh,
'Neath our feet broke the brittle bright stubble like chaff;
Till over by Dalhem a dome-spire sprang white,
And 'Gallop,' gasped Joris, 'for Aix is in sight!'

'How they'll greet us!' – and all in a moment his roan
Rolled neck and croup over, lay dead as a stone;
And there was my Roland to bear the whole weight
Of the news which alone could save Aix from her fate,
With his nostrils like pits full of blood to the brim,
And with circles of red for his eye-sockets' rim.

IX

Then I cast loose my buffcoat, each holster let fall,
Shook off both my jack-boots, let go belt and all,
Stood up in the stirrup, leaned, patted his ear,
Called my Roland his pet-name, my horse without peer;
Clapped my hands, laughed and sang, any noise, bad or good,
Till at length into Aix Roland galloped and stood.

X

And all I remember is, friends flocking round
As I sat with his head 'twixt my knees on the ground;
And no voice but was praising this Roland of mine,
As I poured down his throat our last measure of wine,
Which (the burgesses voted by common consent)
Was no more than his due who brought good news from
    Ghent.

John Bunyan 1628–88

UPON THE SNAIL

She goes but softly, but she goeth sure;
　She stumbles not as stronger creatures do:
Her journey's shorter, so she may endure
　Better than they which do much further go.

She makes no noise, but stilly seizeth on
　The flower or herb appointed for her food,
The which she quietly doth feed upon.
　While others range, and gare, but find no good.

And though she doth but very softly go,
　However 'tis not fast, nor slow, but sure;
And certainly they that do travel so,
　The prize they do aim at they do procure.

Robert Burns 1759–96

TO A MOUSE, ON TURNING HER UP IN HER NEST, WITH THE PLOUGH, NOVEMBER, 1785

Wee, sleeket, cowran, tim'rous beastie,
O, what a panic's in thy breastie!
Thou need na start awa sae hasty,
        Wi' bickering brattle!
I wad be laith to rin an' chase thee,
        Wi' murd'ring pattle!

I'm truly sorry Man's dominion
Has broken Nature's social union,
An' justifies that ill opinion,
        Which makes thee startle,
At me, thy poor, earth-born companion,
        An' fellow-mortal!

I doubt na, whyles, but thou may thieve;
What then? poor beastie, thou maun live!
A daimen-icker in a thrave
        'S a sma' request:
I'll get a blessin wi' the lave,
        An' never miss't!

Thy wee-bit housie, too, in ruin!
It's silly wa's the win's are strewin!
An' naething, now, to big a new ane,
        O' foggage green!
An' bleak December's winds ensuin,
        Baith snell an' keen!

Thou saw the fields laid bare an' wast,
An' weary Winter coming fast,
An' cozie here, beneath the blast,
        Thou thought to dwell,

Till crash! the cruel coulter past
    Out thro' thy cell.

That wee-bit heap o' leaves an' stibble,
Has cost thee monie a weary nibble!
Now thou 's turn'd out, for a' thy trouble,
    But house or hald,
To thole the Winter's sleety dribble,
    An' cranreuch cauld!

But Mousie, thou art no thy-lane,
In proving foresight may be vain:
The best laid schemes o' Mice an' Men,
    Gang aft agley,
An' lea'e us nought but grief an' pain,
    For promis'd joy!

Still, thou art blest, compar'd wi' me!
The present only toucheth thee:
But Och! I backward cast my e'e,
    On prospects drear!
An' forward, tho' I canna see,
    I guess an' fear!

George Gordon, Lord Byron 1788–1824

SO, WE'LL GO NO MORE A ROVING

I

So, we'll go no more a roving
   So late into the night,
Though the heart be still as loving,
   And the moon be still as bright.

II

For the sword outwears its sheath,
   And the soul wears out the breast,
And the heart must pause to breathe,
   And love itself have rest.

III

Though the night was made for loving,
   And the day returns too soon,
Yet we'll go no more a roving
   By the light of the moon.

THE SOLDIER'S DREAM

Our bugles sang truce, for the night-cloud had lower'd.
  And the sentinel stars set their watch in the sky;
And thousands had sunk on the ground overpower'd,
  The weary to sleep, and the wounded to die.

When reposing that night on my pallet of straw
  By the wolf-scaring faggot that guarded the slain,
At the dead of the night a sweet vision I saw;
  And thrice ere the morning I dreamt it again.

Methought from the battle-field's dreadful array
  Far, far I had roam'd on a desolate track:
'Twas autumn, – and sunshine arose on the way
  To the home of my fathers, that welcomed me back.

I flew to the pleasant fields traversed so oft
  In life's morning march, when my bosom was young;
I heard my own mountain-goats bleating aloft,
  And knew the sweet strain that the corn-reapers sung.

Then pledged we the wine-cup, and fondly I swore
  From my home and my weeping friends never to part;
My little ones kiss'd me a thousand times o'er,
  And my wife sobb'd aloud in her fullness of heart.

'Stay – stay with us! – rest! – thou art weary and worn!' –
  And fain was their war-broken soldier to stay; –
But sorrow return'd with the dawning of morn,
  And the voice in my dreaming ear melted away.

SONG

Ask me no more where Jove bestows,
When June is past, the fading rose;
For in your beauty's orient deep
These flowers, as in their causes, sleep.

Ask me no more whither doth stray
The golden atoms of the day;
For in pure love heaven did prepare
Those powders to enrich your hair.

Ask me no more whither doth haste
The nightingale when May is past;
For in your sweet dividing throat
She winters and keeps warm her note.

Ask me no more where those stars light
That downwards fall in dead of night;
For in your eyes they sit, and there
Fixed become as in their sphere.

Ask me no more if east or west
The Phoenix builds her spicy nest;
For unto you at last she flies,
And in your fragrant bosom dies.

FATHER WILLIAM

'You are old, Father William,' the young man said,
  'And your hair has become very white;
And yet you incessantly stand on your head –
  Do you think, at your age, it is right?'

'In my youth,' Father William replied to his son,
  'I feared it might injure the brain;
But, now that I'm perfectly sure I have none,
  Why, I do it again and again.'

'You are old,' said the youth, 'as I mentioned before,
  And have grown most uncommonly fat;
Yet you turned a back-somersault in at the door –
  Pray, what is the reason of that?'

'In my youth,' said the sage, as he shook his grey locks,
  'I kept all my limbs very supple
By the use of this ointment – one shilling the box –
  Allow me to sell you a couple?'

'You are old,' said the youth, 'and your jaws are too weak
  For anything tougher than suet;
Yet you finished the goose, with the bones and the beak –
  Pray, how did you manage to do it?'

'In my youth,' said his father, 'I took to the law,
  And argued each case with my wife;
And the muscular strength, which it gave to my jaw,
  Has lasted the rest of my life.'

'You are old,' said the youth, 'one would hardly suppose
    That your eye was as steady as ever;
Yet you balanced an eel on the end of your nose –
    What made you so awfully clever?'

'I have answered three questions, and that is enough,'
    Said his father; 'don't give yourself airs!
Do you think I can listen all day to such stuff?
    Be off, or I'll kick you down stairs!'

C. P. Cavafy 1863–1933
(Translated by Edmund Keeley and Philip Sherrard)

ITHAKA

As you set out for Ithaka
hope your road is a long one,
full of adventure, full of discovery.
Laistrygonians, Cyclops,
angry Poseidon – don't be afraid of them:
you'll never find things like that on your way
as long as you keep your thoughts raised high,
as long as a rare excitement
stirs your spirit and your body.
Laistrygonians, Cyclops,
wild Poseidon – you won't encounter them
unless you bring them along inside your soul,
unless your soul sets them up in front of you.

Hope your road is a long one.
May there be many summer mornings when,
with what pleasure, what joy,
you enter harbours you're seeing for the first time;
may you stop at Phoenician trading stations
to buy fine things,
mother of pearl and coral, amber and ebony,
sensual perfume of every kind –
as many sensual perfumes as you can;
and may you visit many Egyptian cities
to learn and go on learning from their scholars.

Keep Ithaka always in your mind.
Arriving there is what you're destined for.
But don't hurry the journey at all.
Better if it lasts for years,
so you're old by the time you reach the island,

44

wealthy with all you've gained on the way,
not expecting Ithaka to make you rich.

Ithaka gave you the marvellous journey.
Without her you wouldn't have set out.
She has nothing left to give you now.
And if you find her poor, Ithaka won't have fooled you.
Wise as you will have become, so full of experience,
you'll have understood by then what these Ithakas mean.

G. K. Chesterton 1874–1936

THE ENGLISHMAN

St George he was for England,
And before he killed the dragon
He drank a pint of English ale
Out of an English flagon.
For though he fast right readily
In hair-shirt or in mail,
It isn't safe to give him cakes
Unless you give him ale.

St George he was for England,
And right gallantly set free
The lady left for dragon's meat
And tied up to a tree;
But since he stood for England
And knew what England means,
Unless you give him bacon
You musn't give him beans.

St George he is for England,
And shall wear the shield he wore
When we go out in armour
With the battle-cross before.
But though he is jolly company
And very pleased to dine,
It isn't safe to give him nuts
Unless you give him wine.

John Clare 1793–1864

I AM

Written in Northampton County Asylum

I am – yet what I am, none cares or knows;
　My friends forsake me like a memory lost:
I am the self-consumer of my woes –
　They rise and vanish in oblivions host,
Like shadows in love frenzied stifled throes
　And yet I am, and live – like vapours tost

Into the nothingness of scorn and noise,
　Into the living sea of waking dreams,
Where there is neither sense of life or joys,
　But the vast shipwreck of my lifes esteems;
Even the dearest that I love the best
　Are strange – nay, rather, stranger than the rest.

I long for scenes where man hath never trod
　A place where woman never smiled or wept
There to abide with my Creator God,
　And sleep as I in childhood sweetly slept,
Untroubling and untroubled where I lie
　The grass below, above, the vaulted sky.

Samuel Taylor Coleridge 1772–1834

ANSWER TO A CHILD'S QUESTION

Do you ask what the birds say? The Sparrow, the Dove,
The Linnet and Thrush say, 'I love and I love!'
In the winter they're silent – the wind is so strong;
What it says, I don't know, but it sings a loud song.
But green leaves, and blossoms, and sunny warm weather,
And singing, and loving – all come back together.
But the Lark is so brimful of gladness and love,
The green fields below him, the blue sky above,
That he sings, and he sings; and for ever sings he –
'I love my Love, and my Love loves me!'

Padraic Colum 1881–1972

A CRADLE SONG

O, men from the fields!
Come gently within.
Tread softly, softly,
O! men coming in.

Mavourneen is going
From me and from you,
Where Mary will fold him
With mantle of blue!

From reek of the smoke
And cold of the floor,
And the peering of things
Across the half-door.

O, men from the fields!
Soft, softly come thro'.
Mary puts round him
Her mantle of blue.

William Cowper 1731–1800

THE POPLAR-FIELD

The poplars are felled, farewell to the shade
And the whispering sound of the cool colonnade,
The winds play no longer, and sing in the leaves,
Nor Ouse on his bosom their image receives.

Twelve years have elapsed since I last took a view
Of my favourite field and the bank where they grew,
And now in the grass behold they are laid,
And the tree is my seat that once lent me a shade.

The blackbird has fled to another retreat
Where the hazels afford him a screen from the heat,
And the scene where his melody charmed me before,
Resounds with his sweet-flowing ditty no more.

My fugitive years are all hasting away,
And I must ere long lie as lowly as they,
With a turf on my breast, and a stone at my head,
Ere another such grove shall arise in its stead.

'Tis a sight to engage me, if any thing can,
To muse on the perishing pleasures of man;
Though his life be a dream, his enjoyments, I see,
Have a being less durable even than he.

ANYONE LIVED IN A PRETTY HOW TOWN

anyone lived in a pretty how town
(with up so floating many bells down)
spring summer autumn winter
he sang his didn't he danced his did.

Women and men (both little and small)
cared for anyone not at all
they sowed their isn't they reaped their same
sun moon stars rain

children guessed (but only a few
and down they forgot as up they grew
autumn winter spring summer)
that noone loved him more by more

when by now and tree by leaf
she laughed his joy she cried his grief
bird by snow and stir by still
anyone's any was all to her

someones married their everyones
laughed their cryings and did their dance
(sleep wake hope and then) they
said their nevers they slept their dream

stars rain sun moon
(and only the snow can begin to explain
how children are apt to forget to remember
with up so floating many bells down)

one day anyone died i guess
(and noone stooped to kiss his face)
busy folk buried them side by side
little by little and was by was

all by all and deep by deep
and more by more they dream their sleep
noone and anyone earth by april
wish by spirit and if by yes.

Women and men (both dong and ding)
summer autumn winter spring
reaped their sowing and went their came
sun moon stars rain

John Davidson 1857–1909

A RUNNABLE STAG

When the pods went pop on the broom, green broom,
    And apples began to be golden-skinned,
We harboured a stag in the Priory coomb,
    And we feathered his trail up-wind, up-wind,
    We feathered his trail up-wind –
        A stag of warrant, a stag, a stag,
        A runnable stag, a kingly crop,
        Brow, bay and tray and three on top,
        A stag, a runnable stag.

Then the huntsman's horn rang yap, yap, yap,
    And 'Forwards' we heard the harbourer shout;
But 'twas only a brocket that broke a gap
    In the beechen underwood, driven out,
    From the underwood antlered out
        By warrant and might of the stag, the stag,
        The runnable stag, whose lordly mind
        Was bent on sleep, though beamed and tined
        He stood, a runnable stag.

So we tufted the covert till afternoon
    With Tinkerman's Pup and Bell-of-the–North;
And hunters were sulky and hounds out of tune
    Before we tufted the right stag forth,
    Before we tufted him forth,
        The stag of warrant, the wily stag,
        The runnable stag with his kingly crop,
        Brow, bay and tray and three on top,
        The royal and runnable stag.

It was Bell-of-the–North and Tinkerman's Pup
    That stuck to the scent till the copse was drawn.
'Tally ho! tally ho!' and the hunt was up,

The tufters whipped and the pack laid on,
The resolute pack laid on,
    And the stag of warrant away at last,
    The runnable stag, the same, the same,
    His hoofs on fire, his horns like flame,
    A stag, a runnable stag.

'Let your gelding be: if you check or chide
    He stumbles at once and you're out of the hunt;
For three hundred gentlemen, able to ride,
    On hunters accustomed to bear the brunt,
    Accustomed to bear the brunt,
        Are after the runnable stag, the stag,
        The runnable stag with his kingly crop,
        Brow, bay and tray and three on top,
        The right, the runnable stag.'

By perilous paths in coomb and dell,
    The heather, the rocks, and the river-bed,
The pace grew hot, for the scent lay well,
    And a runnable stag goes right ahead,
    The quarry went right ahead –
        Ahead, ahead, and fast and far;
        His antlered crest, his cloven hoof,
        Brow, bay and tray and three aloof,
        The stag, the runnable stag.

For a matter of twenty miles and more,
    By the densest hedge and the highest wall,
Through herds of bullocks he baffled the lore
    Of harbourer, huntsman, hounds and all,
    Of harbourer hounds and all –
        The stag of warrant, the wily stag,
        For twenty miles, and five and five,
        He ran, and he never was caught alive,
        This stag, this runnable stag.

When he turned at bay in the leafy gloom,
    In the emerald gloom where the brook ran deep,
He heard in the distance the rollers boom,
    And he saw in a vision of peaceful sleep,
    In a wonderful vision of sleep,
        A stag of warrant, a stag, a stag,
        A runnable stag in a jewelled bed,
        Under the sheltering ocean dead,
        A stag, a runnable stag.

So a fateful hope lit up his eye,
    And he opened his nostrils wide again,
And he tossed his branching antlers high
    As he headed the hunt down the Charlock glen,
    As he raced down the echoing glen
        For five miles more, the stag, the stag,
        For twenty miles, and five and five,
        Not to be caught now, dead or alive,
        The stag, the runnable stag.

Three hundred gentlemen, able to ride,
    Three hundred horses as gallant and free,
Beheld him escape on the evening tide,
    Far out till he sank in the Severn Sea,
    Till he sank in the depths of the sea —
        The stag, the buoyant stag, the stag
        That slept at last in a jewelled bed
        Under the sheltering ocean spread,
        The stag, the runnable stag.

THE RAIN

I hear leaves drinking rain;
   I hear rich leaves on top
Giving the poor beneath
   Drop after drop;
'Tis a sweet noise to hear
These green leaves drinking near.

And when the Sun comes out,
   After this rain shall stop,
A wondrous light will fill
   Each dark, round drop;
I hope the Sun shines bright;
'Twill be a lovely sight.

THE GRASS SO LITTLE HAS TO DO

The Grass so little has to do –
A Sphere of simple Green –
With only Butterflies to brood
And Bees to entertain –

And stir all day to pretty Tunes
The Breezes fetch along –
And hold the Sunshine in its lap
And bow to everything –

And thread the Dews, all night, like Pearls –
And make itself so fine
A Duchess were too common
For such a noticing –

And even when it dies – to pass
In Odors so divine –
Like Lowly spices, lain to sleep –
Or Spikenards, perishing –

And then, in Sovereign Barns to dwell –
And dream the Days away,
The Grass so little has to do
I wish I were a Hay –

John Donne 1572–1631

THE SUNNE RISING

Busie old foole, unruly Sunne,
    Why dost thou thus,
Through windowes, and through curtaines call on us?
Must to thy motions lovers seasons run?
    Sawcy pedantique wretch, goe chide
    Late schoole boyes and sowre prentices,
  Goe tell Court-huntsmen, that the King will ride,
  Call countrey ants to harvest offices;
Love, all alike, no season knowes, nor clyme,
Nor houres, dayes, moneths, which are the rags of time.

    Thy beames, so reverend, and strong
    Why shouldst thou thinke?
I could eclipse and cloud them with a winke,
But that I would not lose her sight so long:
    If her eyes have not blinded thine,
    Looke, and to morrow late, tell mee,
  Whether both the'India's of spice and Myne
  Be where thou leftst them, or lie here with mee.
Aske for those Kings whom thou saw'st yesterday,
And thou shalt heare, All here in one bed lay.

    She'is all States, and all Princes, I,
    Nothing else is.
Princes doe but play us; compar'd to this,
All honor's mimique; All wealth alchimie.
    Thou sunne art halfe as happy'as wee,
    In that the world's contracted thus;
  Thine age askes ease, and since thy duties bee
  To warme the world, that's done in warming us.
Shine here to us, and thou art every where;
This bed thy center is, these walls, thy spheare.

Michael Drayton 1563–1631

DEAR, WHY SHOULD YOU COMMAND ME TO MY REST

Dear, why should you command me to my rest,
   When now the night doth summon all to sleep?
Methinks this time becometh lovers best;
   Night was ordained together friends to keep.
How happy are all other living things,
   Which though the day disjoin by several flight,
The quiet evening yet together brings,
   And each returns unto his love at night.
O thou that art so courteous else to all,
   Why shouldst thou, Night, abuse me only thus,
That every creature to his kind dost call,
   And yet 'tis thou dost only sever us?
      Well could I wish it would be ever day,
      If, when night comes, you bid me go away.

MAMBLE

I never went to Mamble
That lies above the Teme,
So I wonder who's in Mamble,
And whether people seem
Who breed and brew along there
As lazy as the name,
And whether any song there
Sets alehouse wits aflame.

The finger-post says Mamble,
And that is all I know
Of the narrow road to Mamble,
And should I turn and go
To that place of lazy token
That lies above the Teme,
There might be a Mamble broken
That was lissom in a dream.

So leave the road to Mamble
And take another road
To as good a place as Mamble
Be it lazy as a toad;
Who travels Worcester county
Takes any place that comes
When April tosses bounty
To the cherries and the plums.

THE IRISH EMIGRANT

I'm sitting on the stile, Mary,
    Where we sat, side by side,
That bright May morning long ago
    When first you were my bride.
The corn was springing fresh and green,
    And the lark sang loud and high,
The red was on your lip, Mary,
    The love-light in your eye.

The place is little changed, Mary,
    The day is bright as then,
The lark's loud song is in my ear,
    The corn is green again;
But I miss the soft clasp of your hand,
    Your breath warm on my cheek,
And I still keep list'ning for the words
    You never more may speak.

'Tis but a step down yonder lane,
    The little Church stands near –
The Church where we were wed, Mary –
    I see the spire from here;
But the graveyard lies between, Mary –
    My step might break your rest –
Where you, my darling, lie asleep
    With your baby on your breast.

I'm very lonely now, Mary –
    The poor make no new friends –
But, oh, they love the better still
    The few our Father sends.
And you were all I had, Mary,
    My blessing and my pride;

There's nothing left to care for now,
    Since my poor Mary died.

Yours was the good brave heart, Mary,
    That still kept hoping on,
When trust in God had left my soul,
    And half my strength was gone.
There was comfort ever on your lip,
    And the kind look on your brow.
I bless you, Mary, for that same,
    Though you can't hear me now.

I thank you for the patient smile
    When your heart was fit to break;
When the hunger pain was gnawing there
    You hid it for my sake!
I bless you for the pleasant word,
    When your heart was sad and sore.
Oh! I'm thankful you are gone, Mary,
    Where grief can't reach you more!

I'm bidding you a long farewell,
    My Mary – kind and true!
But I'll not forget you, darling,
    In the land I'm going to.
They say there's bread and work for all,
    And the sun shines always there;
But I'll not forget old Ireland,
    Were it fifty times as fair!

And when amid those grand old woods
    I sit and shut my eyes,
My heart will travel back again
    To where my Mary lies;
I'll think I see the little stile
    Where we sat, side by side,
And the springing corn and bright May morn,
    When first you were my bride.

LA FIGLIA CHE PIANGE

O quam te memorem virgo . . .

Stand on the highest pavement of the stair —
Lean on a garden urn —
Weave, weave the sunlight in your hair
Clasp your flowers to you with a pained surprise —
Fling them to the ground and turn
With a fugitive resentment in your eyes:
But weave, weave the sunlight in your hair.

So I would have had him leave,
So I would have had her stand and grieve,
So he would have left
As the soul leaves the body torn and bruised,
As the mind deserts the body it has used.
I should find
Some way incomparably light and deft,
Some way we both should understand,
Simple and faithless as a smile and shake of the hand.

She turned away, but with the autumn weather
Compelled my imagination many days,
Many days and many hours:
Her hair over her arms and her arms full of flowers.
And I wonder how they should have been together!
I should have lost a gesture and a pose.
Sometimes these cogitations still amaze
The troubled midnight and the noon's repose.

U. A. Fanthorpe 1929–

NOT MY BEST SIDE

(*Uccello*: S. George and the Dragon, *The National Gallery*)

I

Not my best side, I'm afraid.
The artist didn't give me a chance to
Pose properly, and as you can see,
Poor chap, he had this obsession with
Triangles, so he left off two of my
Feet. I didn't comment at the time
(What, after all, are two feet
To a monster?) but afterwards
I was sorry for the bad publicity.
Why, I said to myself, should my conqueror
Be so ostentatiously beardless, and ride
A horse with a deformed neck and square hoofs?
Why should my victim be so
Unattractive as to be inedible,
And why should she have me literally
On a string? I don't mind dying
Ritually, since I always rise again,
But I should have liked a little more blood
To show they were taking me seriously.

II

It's hard for a girl to be sure if
She wants to be rescued. I mean, I quite
Took to the dragon. It's nice to be
Liked, if you know what I mean. He was
So nicely physical, with his claws
And lovely green skin, and that sexy tail,
And the way he looked at me,
He made me feel he was all ready to

Eat me. And any girl enjoys that.
So when this boy turned up, wearing machinery,
On a really *dangerous* horse, to be honest,
I didn't much fancy him. I mean,
What was he like underneath the hardware?
He might have acne, blackheads or even
Bad breath for all I could tell, but the dragon –
Well, you could see all his equipment
At a glance. Still, what could I do?
The dragon got himself beaten by the boy,
And a girl's got to think of her future.

III

I have diplomas in Dragon
Management and Virgin Reclamation.
My horse is the latest model, with
Automatic transmission and built-in
Obsolescence. My spear is custom-built,
And my prototype armour
Still on the secret list. You can't
Do better than me at the moment.
I'm qualified and equipped to the
Eyebrow. So why be difficult?
Don't you want to be killed and/or rescued
In the the most contemporary way? Don't
You want to carry out the roles
That sociology and myth have designed for you?
Don't you realize that, by being choosy,
You are endangering job-prospects
In the spear- and horse-building industries?
What, in any case, does it matter what
You want? You're in my way.

SONG

I saw a child with silver hair.
Stick with me and I'll take you there.
   Clutch my hand.
   Don't let go.
The fields are mined and the wind blows cold.
The wind blows through his silver hair.

The Blue Vein River is broad and deep.
The branches creak and the shadows leap.
   Clutch my hand.
   Stick to the path.
The fields are mined and the moon is bright.
I saw a child who will never sleep.

Far from the wisdom of the brain
I saw a child grow old in pain.
   Clutch my hand.
   Stay with me.
The fields are mined by the enemy.
Tell me we may be friends again.

Far from the wisdom of the blood
I saw a child reach from the mud.
   Clutch my hand.
   Clutch my heart.
The fields are mined and the moon is dark.
The Blue Vein River is in full flood.

Far from the wisdom of the heart.
I saw a child being torn apart.
   Is this you?
   Is this me?
The fields are mined and the night is long.
Stick with me when the shooting starts.

James Elroy Flecker 1884–1915

TO A POET A THOUSAND YEARS HENCE

I who am dead a thousand years,
   And wrote this sweet archaic song,
Send you my words for messengers
   The way I shall not pass along.

I care not if you bridge the seas,
   Or ride secure the cruel sky,
Or build consummate palaces
   Of metal or of masonry.

But have you wine and music still,
   And statues and a bright-eyed love,
And foolish thoughts of good and ill,
   And prayers to them who sit above?

How shall we conquer? Like a wind
   That falls at eve our fancies blow,
And old Mæonides the blind
   Said it three thousand years ago.

O friend unseen, unborn, unknown,
   Student of our sweet English tongue,
Read out my words at night, alone:
   I was a poet, I was young.

Since I can never see your face,
   And never shake you by the hand,
I send my soul through time and space
   To greet you. You will understand.

THE ROAD NOT TAKEN

Two roads diverged in a yellow wood,
And sorry I could not travel both
And be one traveler, long I stood
And looked down one as far as I could
To where it bent in the undergrowth;

Then took the other, as just as fair,
And having perhaps the better claim,
Because it was grassy and wanted wear;
Though as for that, the passing there
Had worn them really about the same,

And both that morning equally lay
In leaves no step had trodden black.
Oh, I kept the first for another day!
Yet knowing how way leads on to way,
I doubted if I should ever come back.

I shall be telling this with a sigh
Somewhere ages and ages hence:
Two roads diverged in a wood, and I –
I took the one less traveled by,
And that has made all the difference.

Wilfrid Wilson Gibson 1878–1962

SNUG IN MY EASY CHAIR

Snug in my easy chair,
I stirred the fire to flame,
Fantastically fair,
The flickering fancies came,
Born of heart's desire:
Amber woodland streaming;
Topaz islands dreaming;
Sunset-cities gleaming,
Spire on burning spire;
Ruddy-windowed taverns;
Sunshine-spilling wines;
Crystal-lighted caverns
Of Golconda's mines;
Summers, unreturning;
Passion's crater yearning;
Troy, the ever-burning;
Shelley's lustral pyre;
Dragon-eyes, unsleeping;
Witches' caldrons leaping;
Golden galleys sweeping
Out from sea-walled Tyre:
Fancies, fugitive and fair,
Flashed with singing through the air;
Till, dazzled by the drowsy glare,
I shut my eyes to heat and light;
And saw, in sudden night,
Crouched in the dripping dark,
With steaming shoulders stark,
The man who hews the coal to feed my fire.

A. D. Godley 1856–1925

ON THE MOTOR BUS

What is this that roareth thus?
Can it be a Motor Bus?
Yes, the smell and hideous hum
Indicat Motorem Bum!
Implet in the Corn and High
Terror me Motoris Bi:
Bo Motori clamitabo
Ne Motore caedar a Bo –
Dative be or Ablative
So thou only let us live: –
Whither shall thy victims flee?
Spare us, spare us, Motor Be!
Thus I sang; and still anigh
Came in hordes Motores Bi,
Et complebat omne forum
Copia Motorum Borum.
How shall wretches live like us
Cincti Bis Motoribus?
Domine, defende nos
Contra hos Motores Bos!

FLYING CROOKED

The butterfly, a cabbage-white,
(His honest idiocy of flight)
Will never now, it is too late,
Master the art of flying straight,
Yet has – who knows so well as I? –
A just sense of how not to fly:
He lurches here and here by guess
And God and hope and hopelessness.
Even the aerobatic swift
Has not his flying-crooked gift.

Dorothy Frances Gurney 1858–1932

GOD'S GARDEN

The Lord God planted a garden
   In the first white days of the world,
And He set there an angel warden
   In a garment of light enfurled.

So near to the peace of Heaven
   The hawk might nest with the wren,
For there in the cool of the even
   God walked with the first of men.

And I dream that these garden closes
   With their glades and their sun-flecked sod
And their lilies and bowers of roses
   Were laid by the hand of God.

The kiss of the sun for pardon,
   The song of the birds for mirth,
One is nearer God's Heart in a garden
   Than anywhere else on earth.

THE RUINED MAID

'O 'Melia, my dear, this does everything crown!
Who could have supposed I should meet you in Town?
And whence such fair garments, such prosperi-ty?' –
'O didn't you know I'd been ruined?' said she.

– 'You left us in tatters, without shoes or socks,
Tired of digging potatoes, and spudding up docks;
And now you've gay bracelets and bright feathers three!' –
'Yes: that's how we dress when we're ruined,' said she.

– 'At home in the barton you said "thee" and "thou",
And "thik oon", and "theäs oon", and "t'other"; but now
Your talking quite fits 'ee for high compa-ny!' –
'Some polish is gained with one's ruin,' said she.

– 'Your hands were like paws then, your face blue and bleak
But now I'm bewitched by your delicate cheek.
And your little gloves fit as on any la-dy!' –
'We never do work when we're ruined,' said she.

– 'You used to call home-life a hag-ridden dream,
And you'd sigh, and you'd sock; but at present you seem
To know not of megrims or melancho-ly!' –
'True. One's pretty lively when ruined,' said she.

– 'I wish I had feathers, a fine sweeping gown,
And a delicate face, and could strut about Town!' –
'My dear – a raw country girl, such as you be,
Cannot quite expect that. You ain't ruined,' said she.

THE LANDING OF THE PILGRIM FATHERS

The breaking waves dashed high
　　On a stern and rock-bound coast,
And the woods, against a stormy sky,
　　Their giant branches tost:

And the heavy night hung dark
　　The hills and water o'er,
When a band of exiles moored their bark
　　On the wild New England shore.

Not as the conqueror comes,
　　They, the true-hearted, came,
Not with the roll of the stirring drums
　　And the trumpet that sings of fame;

Not as the flying come,
　　In silence and in fear –
They shook the depths of the desert's gloom
　　With their hymns of lofty cheer.

Amidst the storm they sang,
　　And the stars heard and the sea!
And the sounding aisles of the dim woods rang
　　To the anthem of the free.

The ocean-eagle soared
　　From his nest by the white wave's foam,
And the rocking pines of the forest roared –
　　This was their welcome home!

There were men with hoary hair
　　Amidst that pilgrim-band –
Why had they come to wither there,
　　Away from their childhood's land?

There was woman's fearless eye,
    Lit by her deep love's truth;
There was manhood's brow serenely high,
    And the fiery heart of youth.

What sought they thus afar?
    Bright jewels of the mine?
The wealth of seas, the spoils of war? –
    They sought a faith's pure shrine!

Ay, call it holy ground,
    The soil where first they trod!
They have left unstained what there they found –
    Freedom to worship God!

INVICTUS

Out of the night that covers me,
  Black as the pit from pole to pole,
I thank whatever gods may be
  For my unconquerable soul.

In the fell clutch of circumstance
  I have not winced nor cried aloud:
Under the bludgeonings of chance
  My head is bloody, but unbow'd.

Beyond this place of wrath and tears
  Looms but the Horror of the shade,
And yet the menace of the years
  Finds and shall find me unafraid.

It matters not how strait the gate,
  How charged with punishments the scroll,
I am the master of my fate:
  I am the captain of my soul.

Adrian Henri 1932–

TONIGHT AT NOON*

(for Charles Mingus and the Clayton Squares)

Tonight at noon
Supermarkets will advertise 3p EXTRA on everything
Tonight at noon
Children from happy families will be sent to live in a home
Elephants will tell each other human jokes
America will declare peace on Russia
World War I generals will sell poppies in the streets on
    November 11th
The first daffodils of autumn will appear
When the leaves fall upwards to the trees

Tonight at noon
Pigeons will hunt cats through city backyards
Hitler will tell us to fight on the beaches and on the landing
    fields
A tunnel full of water will be built under Liverpool
Pigs will be sighted flying in formation over Woolton
and Nelson will not only get his eye back but his arm as well
White Americans will demonstrate for equal rights
in front of the Black House
and the Monster has just created Dr Frankenstein

Girls in bikinis are moonbathing
Folksongs are being sung by real folk
Artgalleries are closed to people over 21
Poets get their poems in the Top 20
Politicians are elected to insane asylums
There's jobs for everyone and nobody wants them

In back alleys everywhere teenage lovers are kissing
in broad daylight
In forgotten graveyards everywhere the dead will quietly
bury the living
and
You will tell me you love me
Tonight at noon

* *The title of this poem is taken from an LP by Charles Mingus, 'Tonight at Noon', Atlantic 1416.*

George Herbert 1593–1633

THE COLLAR

I struck the board, and cry'd, No more.
                    I will abroad.
What? shall I ever sigh and pine?
My lines and life are free; free as the rode,
          Loose as the winde, as large as store.
                Shall I be still in suit?
          Have I no harvest but a thorn
          To let me bloud, and not restore
What I have lost with cordiall fruit?
                            Sure there was wine
     Before my sighs did drie it: there was corn
                Before my tears did drown it.
          Is the yeare onely lost to me?
                Have I no bayes to crown it?
No flowers, no garlands gay? all blasted?
                          All wasted?
     Not so, my heart: but there is fruit,
                          And thou hast hands.
          Recover all thy sigh-blown age
On double pleasures: leave thy cold dispute
Of what is fit, and not forsake thy cage,
                     Thy rope of sands,
Which pettie thoughts have made, and made to thee
          Good cable, to enforce and draw,
                          And be thy law,
     While thou didst wink and wouldst not see.
                     Away; take heed:
                     I will abroad.
Call in thy deaths head there: tie up thy fears.
                     He that forbears

To suit and serve his need,
                    Deserves his load.
But as I rav'd and grew more fierce and wilde
                    At every word,
Me thoughts I heard one calling, *Child*:
                    And I reply'd, *My Lord*.

TO *ANTHEA*, WHO MAY COMMAND HIM ANY THING

Bid me to live, and I will live
    Thy Protestant to be:
Or bid me love, and I will give
    A loving heart to thee.

A heart as soft, a heart as kind,
    A heart as sound and free,
As in the whole world thou canst find,
    That heart Ile give to thee.

Bid that heart stay, and it will stay,
    To honour thy Decree:
Or bid it languish quite away,
    And't shall doe so for thee.

Bid me to weep, and I will weep,
    While I have eyes to see:
And having none, yet I will keep
    A heart to weep for thee.

Bid me despaire, and Ile despaire,
    Under that *Cypresse* tree:
Or bid me die, and I will dare
    E'en Death, to die for thee.

Thou art my life, my love, my heart,
    The very eyes of me:
And hast command of every part,
    To live and die for thee.

SHE IS FAR FROM THE LAND

Cables entangling her,
Shipspars for mangling her,
Ropes sure of strangling her;
Blocks over-dangling her:
Tiller to batter her,
Topmast to shatter her,
Tobacco to spatter her;
Boreas blustering,
Boatswain quite flustering,
Thunder-clouds mustering
To blast her with sulphur –
If the deep don't engulf her;
Sometimes fear's scrutiny
Pries out a mutiny,
Sniffs conflagration,
Or hints at starvation: –

All the sea-dangers,
Buccaneers, rangers,
Pirates and Salle-men,
Algerine galleymen,
Tornadoes and typhons,
And horrible syphons,
And submarine travels
Thro' roaring sea-navels,
Everything wrong enough,
Long-boat not long enough,
Vessel not strong enough;
Pitch marring frippery,
The deck very slippery,
And the cabin – built sloping,

The Captain a-toping,
And the mate a blasphemer,
That names his Redeemer,
With inward uneasiness;
The cook known by greasiness,
The victuals beslubber'd
Her bed – in a cupboard;
Things of strange christening,
Snatched in her listening,
Blue lights and red lights
And mention of dead-lights,
And shrouds made a theme of,
Things horrid to dream of, –
And *buoys* in the water,
To fear all exhort her;
Her friend no Leander,
Herself no sea-gander,
And ne'er a cork-jacket
On board of the packet!

The breeze still a-stiffening,
The trumpet quite deafening;
Thoughts of repentance,
And doomsday and sentence;
Everything sinister,
Not a church minister, –
Pilot a blunderer,
Coral reefs under her,
Ready to sunder her;
Trunks tipsy-topsy,
The ship in dropsy;
Waves oversurging her,
Sirens a-dirgeing her;
Sharks all expecting her,

Swordfish dissecting her,
Crabs with their hand-vices
Punishing land vices;
Sea-dogs and unicorns,
Things with no puny horns, –
Mermen carnivorous –
'Good Lord, deliver us!'

SPRING

Nothing is so beautiful as Spring –
   When weeds, in wheels, shoot long and lovely and lush;
Thrush's eggs look little low heavens, and thrush
Through the echoing timber does so rinse and wring
The ear, it strikes like lightnings to hear him sing;
   The glassy peartree leaves and blooms, they brush
   The descending blue; that blue is all in a rush
With richness; the racing lambs too have fair their fling.

What is all this juice and all this joy?
   A strain of the earth's sweet being in the beginning
In Eden garden. – Have, get, before it cloy,

   Before it cloud, Christ, lord, and sour with sinning,
Innocent mind and Mayday in girl and boy,
   Most, O maid's child, thy choice and worthy the winning.

A. E. Housman 1859–1936

From 'A SHROPSHIRE LAD'
XL

Into my heart an air that kills
    From yon far country blows:
What are those blue remembered hills,
    What sprires, what farms are those?

That is the land of lost content,
    I see it shining plain,
The happy highways where I went
    And cannot come again.

A MARCH CALF

Right from the start he is dressed in his best –
    his blacks and his whites
Little Fauntleroy – quiffed and glossy,
A Sunday suit, a wedding natty get-up,
Standing in dunged straw

Under cobwebby beams, near the mud wall,
Half of him legs,
Shining-eyed, required nothing more
But that mother's milk come back often.

Everything else is in order, just as it is.
Let the summer skies hold off, for the moment.
This is just as he wants it.
A little at a time, of each new thing, is best.

Too much and too sudden is too frightening –
When I block the light, a bulk from space,
To let him in to his mother for a suck,
He bolts a yard or two, then freezes,

Staring from every hair in all directions,
Ready for the worst, shut up in his hopeful religion,
A little syllogism
With a wet blue-reddish muzzle, for God's thumb.

You see all his hopes bustling
As he reaches between the worn rails towards
The topheavy oven of his mother.
He trembles to grow, stretching his curl-tip tongue –

What did cattle ever find here
To make this dear little fellow
So eager to prepare himself?
He is already in the race, and quivering to win –

87

His new purpled eyeball swivel-jerks
In the elbowing push of his plans.
Hungry people are getting hungrier,
Butchers developing expertise and markets,

But he just wobbles his tail – and glistens
Within his dapper profile
Unaware of how his whole lineage
Has been tied up.

He shivers for feel of the world licking his side.
He is like an ember – one glow
Of lighting himself up
With the fuel of himself, breathing and brightening.

Soon he'll plunge out, to scatter his seething joy,
To be present at the grass,
To be free on the surface of such a wideness,
To find himself himself. To stand. To moo.

LA BELLE DAME SANS MERCI

I

Oh, what can ail thee, knight-at-arms,
    Alone and palely loitering?
The sedge has withered from the lake,
    And no birds sing!

II

Oh, what can ail thee, knight-at-arms,
    So haggard and so woe-begone?
The squirrel's granary is full,
    And the harvest's done.

III

I see a lily on thy brow,
    With anguish moist and fever-dew,
And on thy cheek a fading rose
    Fast withereth too.

IV

I met a lady in the meads
    Full beautiful, a fairy's child,
Her hair was long, her foot was light,
    And her eyes were wild.

V

I made a garland for her head,
    And bracelets too, and fragrant zone;
She looked at me as she did love,
    And made sweet moan.

VI

I set her on my pacing steed,
    And nothing else saw all day long;
For sidelong would she bend, and sing
    A fairy's song.

VII

She found me roots of relish sweet,
    And honey wild, and manna dew;
And sure in language strange she said,
    'I love thee true'.

VIII

She took me to her elfin grot,
    And there she wept, and sighed full sore,
And there I shut her wild wild eyes
    With kisses four.

IX

And there she lulled me asleep,
    And there I dreamed – Ah! woe betide! –
The latest dream I ever dreamt
    On the cold hill side.

X

I saw pale kings, and princes too,
    Pale warriors, death-pale were they all;
They cried – 'La belle Dame sans merci
    Thee hath in thrall!'

XI

I saw their starved lips in the gloam
    With horrid warning gapèd wide,
And I awoke, and found me here
    On the cold hill's side.

XII

And this is why I sojourn here,
   Alone and palely loitering,
Though the sedge is withered from the lake,
   And no birds sing.

ODE TO THE NORTH-EAST WIND

Welcome, wild North-easter!
  Shame it is to see
Odes to every zephyr;
  Ne'er a verse to thee.
Welcome, black North-easter!
  O'er the German foam;
O'er the Danish moorlands,
  From thy frozen home.
Tired we are of summer,
  Tired of gaudy glare,
Showers soft and steaming,
  Hot and breathless air.
Tired of listless dreaming,
  Through the lazy day:
 Jovial wind of winter,
  Turn us out to play!
Sweep the golden reed-beds;
  Crisp the lazy dyke;
Hunger into madness
  Every plunging pike.
Fill the lake with wild-fowl;
  Fill the marsh with snipe;
While on dreary moorlands
  Lonely curlew pipe.
Through the black fir-forest
  Thunder harsh and dry,
Shattering down the snow-flakes
  Off the curdled sky.
Hark! The brave North-easter!
  Breast-high lies the scent,
On by holt and headland,
  Over heath and bent.

Chime, ye dappled darlings,
  Through the sleet and snow.
Who can over-ride you?
  Let the horses go!
Chime, ye dappled darlings,
  Down the roaring blast;
You shall see a fox die
  Ere an hour be past.
Go! and rest to-morrow,
  Hunting in your dreams,
While our skates are ringing
  O'er the frozen streams.
Let the luscious South-wind
  Breathe in lovers' sighs
While the lazy gallants
  Bask in ladies' eyes.
What does he but soften
  Heart alike and pen?
'Tis the hard grey weather
  Breeds hard English men.
What's the soft South-wester?
  'Tis the ladies' breeze,
Bringing home their trueloves
  Out of all the seas:
But the black North-easter,
  Through the snow-storm hurled,
Drives our English hearts of oak
  Seaward round the world.
Come, as came our fathers,
  Heralded by thee,
Conquering from the eastward,
  Lords by land and sea.
Come; and strong within us
  Stir the Vikings' blood;
Bracing brain and sinew;
  Blow, thou wind of God!

Rudyard Kipling 1865–1936

IF –

('Brother Square-Toes' – *Rewards and Fairies*)

If you can keep your head when all about you
  Are losing theirs and blaming it on you,
If you can trust yourself when all men doubt you,
  But make allowance for their doubting too;
If you can wait and not be tired by waiting,
  Or being lied about, don't deal in lies,
Or being hated, don't give way to hating,
  And yet don't look too good, nor talk too wise:

If you can dream – and not make dreams your master;
  If you can think – and not make thoughts your aim;
If you can meet with Triumph and Disaster
  And treat those two impostors just the same;
If you can bear to hear the truth you've spoken
  Twisted by knaves to make a trap for fools,
Or watch the things you gave your life to, broken,
  And stoop and build 'em up with worn-out tools:

If you can make one heap of all your winnings
  And risk it on one turn of pitch-and-toss,
And lose, and start again at your beginnings
  And never breathe a word about your loss;
If you can force your heart and nerve and sinew
  To serve your turn long after they are gone,
And so hold on when there is nothing in you
  Except the Will which says to them: 'Hold on!'

If you can talk with crowds and keep your virtue,
　Or walk with Kings – nor lose the common touch,
If neither foes nor loving friends can hurt you,
　If all men count with you, but none too much;
If you can fill the unforgiving minute
　With sixty seconds' worth of distance run,
Yours is the Earth and everything that's in it,
　And – which is more – you'll be a Man, my son!

AN ARUNDEL TOMB

Side by side, their faces blurred,
The earl and countess lie in stone,
Their proper habits vaguely shown
As jointed armour, stiffened pleat,
And that faint hint of the absurd –
The little dogs under their feet.

Such plainness of the pre-baroque
Hardly involves the eye, until
It meets his left-hand gauntlet, still
Clasped empty in the other; and
One sees, with a sharp tender shock,
His hand withdrawn, holding her hand.

They would not think to lie so long.
Such faithfulness in effigy
Was just a detail friends would see:
A sculptor's sweet commissioned grace
Thrown off in helping to prolong
The Latin names around the base.

They would not guess how early in
Their supine stationary voyage
The air would change to soundless damage,
Turn the old tenantry away;
How soon succeeding eyes begin
To look, not read. Rigidly they

Persisted, linked, through lengths and breadths
Of time. Snow fell, undated. Light
Each summer thronged the glass. A bright
Litter of birdcalls strewed the same
Bone-riddled ground. And up the paths
The endless altered people came,

Washing at their identity.
Now, helpless in the hollow of
An unarmorial age, a trough
Of smoke in slow suspended skeins
Above their scrap of history,
Only an attitude remains:

Time has transfigured them into
Untruth. The stone fidelity
They hardly meant has come to be
Their final blazon, and to prove
Our almost-instinct almost true:
What will survive of us is love.

PIANO

Softly, in the dusk, a woman is singing to me;
Taking me back down the vista of years, till I see
A child sitting under the piano, in the boom of the tingling
    strings
And pressing the small, poised feet of a mother who smiles as
    she sings.

In spite of myself, the insidious mastery of song
Betrays me back, till the heart of me weeps to belong
To the old Sunday evenings at home, with winter outside
And hymns in the cosy parlour, the tinkling piano our guide.

So now it is vain for the singer to burst into clamour
With the great black piano appassionato. The glamour
Of childish days is upon me, my manhood is cast
Down in the flood of remembrance, I weep like a child for
    the past.

APRIL RISE

If ever I saw blessing in the air
   I see it now in this still early day
Where lemon-green the vaporous morning drips
   Wet sunlight on the powder of my eye.

Blown bubble-film of blue, the sky wraps round
   Weeds of warm light whose every root and rod
Splutters with soapy green, and all the world
   Sweats with the bead of summer in its bud.

If ever I heard blessing it is there
   Where birds in trees that shoals and shadows are
Splash with their hidden wings and drops of sound
   Break on my ears their crests of throbbing air.

Pure in the haze the emerald sun dilates,
   The lips of sparrows milk the mossy stones,
While white as water by the lake a girl
   Swims her green hand among the gathered swans.

Now, as the almond burns its smoking wick,
   Dropping small flames to light the candled grass;
Now, as my low blood scales its second chance,
   If ever world were blessèd, now it is.

TO A TIMID LEECH

Nay, start not from the banquet where the red wine foams for
    thee,
Though somewhat thick to perforate this epidermis be,
'Tis madness, when the bowl invites to linger at the brink;
So haste thee, haste thee, timid one. Drink, pretty creature,
    drink!

I tell thee, if these azure veins could boast the regal wine
Of Tudors or Plantagenets, the draught should still be thine!
Though round the goblet's beaded brim plebeian bubbles
    wink,
'Twill cheer and not inebriate. Drink, pretty creature, drink!

Perchance, reluctant being, I have placed thee wrong side up,
And the lips that I am chiding have been farthest from the
    cup.
I have waited long and vainly, and I cannot, cannot think
Thou would'st spurn the oft-repeated call: Drink, pretty
    creature, drink!

While I watch'd thy patient struggles, and imagined thou wert
    coy,
'Twas thy tail, and not thy features, that refused the proffer'd
    joy.
I will but turn thee tenderly – nay, never, never shrink –
Now, once again the banquet calls: Drink, pretty creature,
    drink!

Peter Leyland 1909–78

TO A CAT IN A PICTURE GALLERY

A flurry of snow-flakes,
  And out of the street –
Grey paws and grey body –
You came through the doorway
  To sprawl at my feet.

That Umbrian Madonna
  With mantle of blue
By your grey became brighter,
Mantegna's vermilion
  More brilliant for you.

Nuzzling delightedly,
  Cheek, ear and nose
Cold on my warm hand,
Your eyes of soft amber
  With pleasure half-close.

If I see with what rapture
  You stroke your own head
On pretence of caressing me,
Under these paintings
  What more can be said?

Can I doubt that toward Nature
  They followed your plan,
These men who made much of her,
Using her grandeur
  To magnify man?

Clearer the flesh glows.
  Lovelier the face,
For the river that sinuous
Winds, or the shadowland
  Arched in blue space.

For this the brush laboured,
  The mind had delight,
The trees took their colour,
The mountains grew sharper,
  The sky dimmed her light.

How can I laugh at you,
  Cat, as you purr,
With this human to help you
In tickling your ear-roots
  And smoothing your fur?

Vachel Lindsay 1879–1931

THE FLOWER-FED BUFFALOES

The flower-fed buffaloes of the spring
In the days of long ago,
Ranged where the locomotives sing
And the prairie flowers lie low: –
The tossing, blooming, perfumed grass
Is swept away by the wheat,
Wheels and wheels and wheels spin by
In the spring that still is sweet.
But the flower-fed buffaloes of the spring
Left us, long ago.
They gore no more, they bellow no more,
They trundle around the hills no more: –
With the Blackfeet, lying low,
With the Pawnees, lying low,
Lying low.

Henry Wadsworth Longfellow 1807–82

HIAWATHA'S DEPARTURE
From 'THE SONG OF HIAWATHA'

Heavy with the heat and silence
Grew the afternoon of Summer;
With a drowsy sound the forest
Whispered round the sultry wigwam.
With a sound of sleep the water
Rippled on the beach below it;
From the cornfields shrill and ceaseless
Sang the grasshopper, Pah-puk-keena;
And the guests of Hiawatha,
Weary with the heat of Summer,
Slumbered in the sultry wigwam.

Slowly, o'er the simmering landscape
Fell the evening's dusk and coolness,
And the long and level sunbeams
Shot their spears into the forest,
Breaking through its shields of shadow,
Rushed into each secret ambush,
Searched each thicket, dingle, hollow;
Still the guests of Hiawatha
Slumbered in the silent wigwam.

From his place rose Hiawatha,
Bade farewell to old Nokomis,
Spake in whispers, spake in this wise,
Did not wake the guests, that slumbered:

'I am going, O Nokomis,
On a long and distant journey,
To the portals of the Sunset,
To the regions of the home-wind,
Of the Northwest wind, Keewaydin.
But these guests I leave behind me,
In your watch and ward I leave them;

See that never harm comes near them,
See that never fear molests them,
Never danger nor suspicion,
Never want of food or shelter,
In the lodge of Hiawatha!'

    Forth into the village went he,
Bade farewell to all the warriors,
Bade farewell to all the young men,
Spake persuading, spake in this wise:

    'I am going, O my people,
On a long and distant journey;
Many moons and many winters
Will have come, and will have vanished,
Ere I come again to see you.
But my guests I leave behind me;
Listen to their words of wisdom,
Listen to the truth they tell you,
For the Master of Life has sent them
From the land of light and morning!'

    On the shore stood Hiawatha,
Turned and waved his hands at parting;
On the clear and luminous water
Launched his birch canoe for sailing,
From the pebbles of the margin
Shoved it forth into the water;
Whispered to it, 'Westward! westward!'
And with speed it darted forward.

    And the evening sun descending
Set the clouds on fire with redness,
Burned the broad sky, like a prairie,
Left upon the level water
One long track and trail of splendour,
Down whose stream, as down a river,
Westward, westward Hiawatha
Sailed into the fiery sunset,
Sailed into the purple vapours,

Sailed into the dusk of evening.

And the people from the margin
Watched him floating, rising, sinking,
Till the birch canoe seemed lifted
High into that sea of splendour,
Till it sank into the vapours
Like the new moon slowly, slowly
Sinking in the purple distance.

And they said, 'Farewell for ever!'
Said, 'Farewell, O Hiawatha!'
And the forests, dark and lonely,
Moved through all their depths of darkness,
Sighed, 'Farewell, O Hiawatha!'
And the waves upon the margin
Rising, rippling on the pebbles,
Sobbed, 'Farewell, O Hiawatha!'
And the heron, the Shuh-shuh-gah,
From her haunts among the fenlands
Screamed, 'Farewell, O Hiawatha!'

Thus departed Hiawatha!
Hiawatha the Beloved,
In the glory of the sunset,
In the purple mists of evening,
To the regions of the home-wind,
Of the Northwest wind, Keewaydin,
To the Islands of the Blessed,
To the Kingdom of Ponemah,
To the land of the Hereafter!

George MacBeth 1932–92

THE MINER'S HELMET

My father wore it working coal at Shotts
When I was one. My mother stirred his broth
And rocked my cradle with her shivering hands
While this black helmet's long-lost miner's-lamp
Showed him the road home. Through miles of coal
His fragile skull, filled even then with pit-props,
Lay in a shell, the brain's blue-printed future
Warm in its womb. From sheaves of saved brown paper,
Baring an oval into weeks of dust,
I pull it down: its laced straps move to admit
My larger brows; like an abdicated king's
Gold crown of thirty years ago, I touch it
With royal fingers, feel its image firm –
Hands grown to kings' hands calloused on the pick,
Feet slow like kings' feet on the throneward gradient
Up to the coal-face – but the image blurs
Before it settles: there were no crusades.
My father died a draughtsman, drawing plans
In an airy well-lit office above the ground
Beneath which his usurpers, other kings,
Reigned by the fallen helmet he resigned
Which I inherit as a concrete husk.
I hand it back to gather dust on the shelf.

SNOW

The room was suddenly rich and the great bay-window was
Spawning snow and pink roses against it
Soundlessly collateral and incompatible:
World is suddener than we fancy it.

World is crazier and more of it than we think,
Incorrigibly plural. I peel and portion
A tangerine and spit the pips and feel
The drunkenness of things being various.

And the fire flames with a bubbling sound for world
Is more spiteful and gay than one supposes –
On the tongue on the eyes on the ears in the palms of one's
   hands –
There is more than glass between the snow and the huge
   roses.

Derek Mahon 1941–

A DISUSED SHED IN CO. WEXFORD

Let them not forget us, the weak souls among the asphodels.
                    – Seferis, *Mythistorema*

for J. G. Farrell

Even now there are places where a thought might grow –
Peruvian mines, worked out and abandoned
To a slow clock of condensation,
An echo trapped for ever, and a flutter
Of wildflowers in the lift-shaft,
Indian compounds where the wind dances
And a door bangs with diminished confidence,
Lime crevices behind rippling rainbarrels,
Dog corners for bone burials;
And in a disused shed in Co. Wexford,

Deep in the grounds of a burnt-out hotel,
Among the bathtubs and the washbasins
A thousand mushrooms crowd to a keyhole.
This is the one star in their firmament
Or frames a star within a star.
What should they do there but desire?
So many days beyond the rhododendrons
With the world waltzing in its bowl of cloud,
They have learnt patience and silence
Listening to the rooks querulous in the high wood.

They have been waiting for us in a foetor
Of vegetable sweat since civil war days,
Since the gravel-crunching, interminable departure
Of the expropriated mycologist.
He never came back, and light since then
Is a keyhole rusting gently after rain.
Spiders have spun, flies dusted to mildew

And once a day, perhaps, they have heard something –
A trickle of masonry, a shout from the blue
Or a lorry changing gear at the end of the lane.

There have been deaths, the pale flesh flaking
Into the earth that nourished it;
And nightmares, born of these and the grim
Dominion of stale air and rank moisture.
Those nearest the door grow strong –
'Elbow room! Elbow room!'
The rest, dim in a twilight of crumbling
Utensils and broken pitchers, groaning
For their deliverance, have been so long
Expectant that there is left only the posture.

A half century, without visitors, in the dark –
Poor preparation for the cracking lock
And creak of hinges. Magi, moonmen,
Powdery prisoners of the old regime,
Web-throated, stalked like triffids, racked by drought
And insomnia, only the ghost of a scream
At the flash-bulb firing squad we wake them with
Shows there is life yet in their feverish forms.
Grown beyond nature now, soft food for worms,
They lift frail heads in gravity and good faith.

They are begging us, you see, in their wordless way,
To do something, to speak on their behalf
Or at least not to close the door again.
Lost people of Treblinka and Pompeii!
'Save us, save us,' they seem to say,
'Let the god not abandon us
Who have come so far in darkness and in pain.
We too had our lives to live.
You with your light meter and relaxed itinerary,
Let not our naive labours have been in vain!'

110

Walter de la Mare 1873–1956

THE LISTENERS

'Is there anybody there?' said the Traveller,
   Knocking on the moonlit door;
And his horse in the silence champed the grasses
   Of the forest's ferny floor:
And a bird flew up out of the turret,
   Above the Traveller's head:
And he smote upon the door again a second time;
   'Is there anybody there?' he said.
But no one descended to the Traveller;
   No head from the leaf-fringed sill
Leaned over and looked into his grey eyes,
   Where he stood perplexed and still.
But only a host of phantom listeners
   That dwelt in the lone house then
Stood listening in the quiet of the moonlight
   To that voice from the world of men:
Stood thronging the faint moonbeams on the dark stair,
   That goes down to the empty hall,
Hearkening in an air stirred and shaken
   By the lonely Traveller's call.
And he felt in his heart their strangeness,
   Their stillness answering his cry,
While his horse moved, cropping the dark turf,
   'Neath the starred and leafy sky;
For he suddenly smote on the door, even
   Louder, and lifted his head: –
'Tell them I came, and no one answered,
   That I kept my word,' he said.
Never the least stir made the listeners,
   Though every word he spake
Fell echoing through the shadowiness of the still house

From the one man left awake:
Ay, they heard his foot upon the stirrup,
    And the sound of iron on stone,
And how the silence surged softly backward,
    When the plunging hoofs were gone.

THE PASSIONATE SHEPHERD TO HIS LOVE

Come live with me and be my Love,
And we will all the pleasures prove
That hills and valleys, dales and fields,
Or woods or steepy mountain yields.

And we will sit upon the rocks,
And see the shepherds feed their flocks
By shallow rivers, to whose falls
Melodious birds sing madrigals.

And I will make thee beds of roses
And a thousand fragrant posies;
A cap of flowers, and a kirtle
Embroider'd all with leaves of myrtle.

A gown made of the finest wool
Which from our pretty lambs we pull;
Fair-linèd slippers for the cold,
With buckles of the purest gold.

A belt of straw and ivy-buds
With coral clasps and amber studs:
And if these pleasures may thee move,
Come live with me and be my Love.

The shepherd swains shall dance and sing
For thy delight each May morning:
If these delights thy mind may move,
Then live with me and be my Love.

Andrew Marvell 1621–78

TO HIS COY MISTRESS

Had we but world enough, and time,
This coyness, Lady, were no crime.
We would sit down, and think which way
To walk, and pass our long love's day.
Thou by the Indian Ganges' side
Shouldst rubies find: I by the tide
Of Humber would complain. I would
Love you ten years before the flood:
And you should, if you please, refuse
Till the conversion of the Jews.
My vegetable love should grow
Vaster than empires, and more slow.
An hundred years should go to praise
Thine eyes, and on thy forehead gaze.
Two hundred to adore each breast:
But thirty thousand to the rest.
An age at least to every part,
And the last age should show your heart:
For, Lady, you deserve this state;
Nor would I love at lower rate.
    But at my back I always hear
Time's wingèd chariot hurrying near:
And yonder all before us lie
Deserts of vast eternity.
Thy beauty shall no more be found;
Nor, in thy marble vault, shall sound
My echoing song: then worms shall try
That long-preserved virginity:
And your quaint honour turn to dust;
And into ashes all my lust.
The grave's a fine and private place,
But none, I think, do there embrace.

Now, therefore, while the youthful glue
Sits on thy skin like morning dew,
And while thy willing soul transpires
At every pore with instant fires,
Now let us sport us while we may;
And now, like amorous birds of prey,
Rather at once our time devour,
Than languish in his slow-chapped power.
Let us roll all our strength, and all
Our sweetness, up into one ball:
And tear our pleasures with rough strife,
Thorough the iron grates of life.
Thus, though we cannot make our sun
Stand still, yet we will make him run.

ON GROWING OLD

Be with me, Beauty, for the fire is dying;
My dog and I are old, too old for roving.
Man, whose young passion sets the spindrift flying,
Is soon too lame to march, too cold for loving.
I take the book and gather to the fire,
Turning old yellow leaves; minute by minute
The clock ticks to my heart. A withered wire,
Moves a thin ghost of music in the spinet.
I cannot sail your seas, I cannot wander
Your cornland, nor your hill-land, nor your valleys
Ever again, nor share the battle yonder
Where the young knight the broken squadron rallies.
Only stay quiet while my mind remembers
The beauty of fire from the beauty of embers.

Beauty, have pity! for the strong have power,
The rich their wealth, the beautiful their grace,
Summer of man is sunlight and its flower,
Spring-time of man all April in a face.
Only, as in the jostling in the Strand,
Where the mob thrusts or loiters or is loud,
The beggar with the saucer in his hand
Asks only a penny from the passing crowd,
So, from this glittering world with all its fashion,
Its fire, and play of men, its stir, its march,
Let me have wisdom, Beauty, wisdom and passion,
Bread to the soul, rain where the summers parch.
Give me but these, and, though the darkness close
Even the night will blossom as the rose.

Charlotte Mew 1869–1928

OLD SHEPHERD'S PRAYER

Up to the bed by the window, where I be lyin',
Comes bells and bleat of the flock wi' they two children's
clack.
Over, from under the eaves there's the starlings flyin',
And down in yard, fit to burst his chain, yapping out at Sue I
do hear young Mac.

Turning around like a falled-over sack
I can see team ploughin' in Whithy-bush field and meal carts
startin' up road to Church-Town;
Saturday arternoon the men goin' back
And the women from market, trapin' home over the down.

Heavenly Master, I wud like to wake to they same green places
Where I be know'd for breakin' dogs and follerin' sheep.
And if I may not walk in th' old ways and look on th' old
faces
I wud sooner sleep.

Edna St Vincent Millay 1892–1950

RECUERDO

We were very tired, we were very merry –
We had gone back and forth all night on the ferry.
It was bare and bright, and smelled like a stable –
But we looked into a fire, we leaned across a table,
We lay on a hill-top underneath the moon;
And the whistles kept blowing, and the dawn came soon.

We were very tired, we were very merry –
We had gone back and forth all night on the ferry;
And you ate an apple, and I ate a pear,
From a dozen of each we had bought somewhere;
And the sky went wan, and the wind came cold,
And the sun rose dripping, a bucketful of gold.

We were very tired, we were very merry,
We had gone back and forth all night on the ferry.
We hailed, 'Good morrow, mother!' to a shawl-covered head,
And bought a morning paper, which neither of us read;
And she wept, 'God bless you!' for the apples and pears,
And we gave her all our money but our subway fares.

A. A. Milne 1882–1956

KING JOHN'S CHRISTMAS

King John was not a good man –
  He had his little ways.
And sometimes no one spoke to him
  For days and days and days.
And men who came across him,
  When walking in the town,
Gave him a supercilious stare,
Or passed with noses in the air –
And bad King John stood dumbly there,
  Blushing beneath his crown.

King John was not a good man,
  And no good friends had he.
He stayed in every afternoon . . .
  But no one came to tea.
And, round about December,
  The cards upon his shelf
Which wished him lots of Christmas cheer,
And fortune in the coming year,
Were never from his near and dear,
  But only from himself.

King John was not a good man,
  Yet had his hopes and fears.
They'd given him no present now
  For years and years and years.
But every year at Christmas,
  While minstrels stood about,
Collecting tribute from the young
For all the songs they might have sung,
He stole away upstairs and hung
  A hopeful stocking out.

King John was not a good man,
    He lived his life aloof;
Alone he thought a message out
    While climbing up the roof.
He wrote it down and propped it
    Against the chimney stack:
'TO ALL AND SUNDRY – NEAR AND FAR –
F. CHRISTMAS IN PARTICULAR.'
And signed it not 'Johannes R.'
    But very humbly, 'JACK.'

'I want some crackers,
    And I want some candy;
I think a box of chocolates
    Would come in handy;
I don't mind oranges,
    I do like nuts!
And I SHOULD like a pocket-knife
    That really cuts.
And, oh! Father Christmas, if you love me at all,
Bring me a big, red india-rubber ball!'

King John was not a good man –
    He wrote this message out,
And gat him to his room again,
    Descending by the spout.
And all that night he lay there,
    A prey to hopes and fears.
'I think that's him a-coming now,'
    (Anxiety bedewed his brow.)
'He'll bring one present, anyhow –
    The first I've had for years.'

'Forget about the crackers,
    And forget about the candy;
I'm sure a box of chocolates
    Would never come in handy;

I don't like oranges,
   I don't want nuts,
And I HAVE got a pocket-knife
   That almost cuts.
But, oh! Father Christmas, if you love me at all,
Bring me a big, red india-rubber ball!'

King John was not a good man –
   Next morning when the sun
Rose up to tell a waiting world
   That Christmas had begun,
And people seized their stockings,
   And opened them with glee,
And crackers, toys and games appeared,
And lips with sticky sweets were smeared,
King John said grimly: 'As I feared,
   Nothing again for me!'

'I did want crackers,
   And I did want candy;
I know a box of chocolates
   Would come in handy;
I do love oranges,
   I did want nuts.
I haven't got a pocket-knife –
   Not one that cuts.
And, oh! if Father Christmas had loved me at all,
He would have brought a big, red india-rubber ball!'

King John stood by the window,
   And frowned to see below
The happy bands of boys and girls
   All playing in the snow.
A while he stood there watching,
   And envying them all . . .
When through the window big and red
There hurtled by his royal head,

And bounced and fell upon the bed,
　　An india-rubber ball!

AND OH, FATHER CHRISTMAS,
　　MY BLESSINGS ON YOU FALL
　　　　FOR BRINGING HIM
　　　　A BIG, RED,
　　　　INDIA-RUBBER
　　　　BALL!

John Milton 1608–74

ON TIME

Fly envious *Time*, till thou run out thy race,
Call on the lazy leaden-stepping hours,
Whose speed is but the heavy Plummets pace;
And glut thy self with what thy womb devours,
Which is no more than what is false and vain,
And merely mortal dross;
So little is our loss,
So little is thy gain.
For when as each thing bad thou hast entomb'd,
And last of all, thy greedy self consum'd,
Then long Eternity shall greet our bliss
With an individual kiss;
And Joy shall overtake us as a flood,
When every thing that is sincerely good
And perfetly divine,
With Truth, and Peace, and Love shall ever shine
About the supreme Throne
Of him, t'whose happy-making sight alone,
When once our heav'nly guided soul shall clime,
Then all this Earthy grossness quit,
Attir'd with Stars, we shall for ever sit,
　　Triumphing over Death, and Chance, and thee O Time.

THE LIGHT OF OTHER DAYS

Oft, in the stilly night,
   Ere slumber's chain has bound me,
Fond Memory brings the light
   Of other days around me:
   The smiles, the tears
   Of boyhood's years,
   The words of love then spoken;
    The eyes that shone,
    Now dimmed and gone,
   The cheerful hearts now broken!
Thus, in the stilly night,
   Ere slumber's chain has bound me,
Sad Memory brings the light
   Of other days around me.

When I remember all
   The friends, so linked together,
I've seen around me fall
   Like leaves in wintry weather,
   I feel like one
   Who treads alone
   Some banquet-hall deserted,
    Whose lights are fled,
    Whose garlands dead,
   And all but he departed!
Thus, in the stilly night,
   Ere slumber's chain has bound me.
Sad Memory brings the light
   Of other days around me.

William Morris 1834–96

THE END OF MAY

How the wind howls this morn
About the end of May,
And drives June on apace
To mock the world forlorn
And the world's joy passed away
And my unlonged-for face!
The world's joy passed away;
For no more may I deem
That any folk are glad
To see the dawn of day
Sunder the tangled dream
Wherein no grief they had.
Ah, through the tangled dream
Where others have no grief
Ever it fares with me
That fears and treasons stream
And dumb sleep slays belief
Whatso therein may be.
Sleep slayeth all belief
Until the hopeless light
Wakes at the birth of June
More lying tales to weave,
More love in woe's despite,
More hope to perish soon.

Andrew Motion 1952–

ANNE FRANK HUIS

Even now, after twice her lifetime of grief
and anger in the very place, whoever comes
to climb these narrow stairs, discovers how
the bookcase slides aside, then walks through
shadow into sunlit rooms, can never help

but break her secrecy again. Just listening
is a kind of guilt: the Westerkirk repeats
itself outside, as if all time worked round
towards her fear, and made each stroke
die down on guarded streets. Imagine it –

three years of whispering and loneliness
and plotting, day by day, the Allied line
in Europe with a yellow chalk. What hope
she had for ordinary love and interest
survives her here, displayed above the bed

as pictures of her family; some actors;
fashions chosen by Princess Elizabeth.
And those who stoop to see them find
not only patience missing its reward,
but one enduring wish for chances

like my own: to leave as simply
as I do, and walk at ease
up dusty tree-lined avenues, or watch
a silent barge come clear of bridges
settling their reflections in the blue canal.

Edwin Muir 1887–1959

THE CONFIRMATION

Yes, yours, my love, is the right human face.
I in my mind had waited for this long,
Seeing the false and searching for the true,
Then found you as a traveller finds a place
Of welcome suddenly amid the wrong
Valleys and rocks and twisting roads. But you,
What shall I call you? A fountain in a waste,
A well of water in a country dry,
Or anything that's honest and good, an eye
That makes the whole world bright. Your open heart,
Simple with giving, gives the primal deed,
The first good world, the blossom, the blowing seed,
The hearth, the steadfast land, the wandering sea,
Not beautiful or rare in every part,
But like yourself, as they were meant to be.

Lady Caroline Norton 1808–77

BINGEN ON THE RHINE

A soldier of the Legion lay dying in Algiers,
There was lack of woman's nursing, there was dearth of
    woman's tears;
But a comrade stood beside him, while his life-blood ebbed
    away,
And bent, with pitying glances, to hear what he might say.
The dying soldier faltered, as he took that comrade's hand,
And he said, 'I nevermore shall see my own, my native land;
Take a message, and a token, to some distant friends of mine,
For I was born at Bingen, – at Bingen on the Rhine.

'Tell my brothers and companions, when they meet and crowd
    around,
To hear my mournful story, in the pleasant vineyard ground,
That we fought the battle bravely, and when the day was
    done,
Full many a corpse lay ghastly pale beneath the setting sun:
And, 'mid the dead and dying, were some grown old in wars, –
The death-wound on their gallant breasts, the last of many
    scars;
And some were young, and suddenly beheld life's morn
    decline, –
And one had come from Bingen, – fair Bingen on the Rhine.

'Tell my mother that her other sons shall comfort her old age;
For I was aye a truant bird, that thought his home a cage;
For my father was a soldier, and even as a child
My heart leaped forth to hear him tell of struggles fierce and
    wild;
And when he died, and left us to divide his scanty hoard,
I let them take whate'er they would, – but kept my father's
    sword;

And with boyish love I hung it where the bright light used to
  shine,
On the cottage wall at Bingen, – calm Bingen on the Rhine.

'Tell my sister not to weep for me, and sob with drooping
  head,
When the troops come marching home again with glad and
  gallant tread,
But to look upon them proudly, with a calm and steadfast eye,
For her brother was a soldier too, and not afraid to die;
And if a comrade seek her love, I ask her in my name
To listen to him kindly, without regret or shame,
And to hang the old sword in its place (my father's sword and
  mine),
For the honour of old Bingen – dear Bingen on the Rhine.

'There's another, – not a sister; in the happy days gone by
You'd have known her by the merriment that sparkled in her
  eye;
Too innocent for coquetry, – too fond for idle scorning, –
O friend! I fear the lightest heart makes sometimes heaviest
  mourning!
Tell her the last night of my life (for, ere the moon be risen,
My body will be out of pain, my soul be out of prison), –
I dreamed I stood with *her*, and saw the yellow sunlight shine
On the vine-clad hills of Bingen, – fair Bingen on the Rhine.

'I saw the blue Rhine sweep along, – I heard, or seemed to
  hear,
The German songs we used to sing, in chorus sweet and clear;
And down the pleasant river, and up the slanting hill,
The echoing chorus sounded, through the evening calm and
  still;
And her glad blue eyes were on me, as we passed, with
  friendly talk,
Down many a path beloved of yore, and well-remembered
  walk,

And her little hand lay lightly, confidingly in mine, –
But we'll meet no more at Bingen, – loved Bingen on the
  Rhine.'

His trembling voice grew faint and hoarse, – his grasp was
  childish weak, –
His eyes put on a dying look, – he sighed and ceased to speak;
His comrade bent to lift him, but the spark of life had fled, –
The soldier of the Legion in a foreign land was dead!
And the soft moon rose up slowly, and calmly she looked
  down
On the red sand of the battle-field, with bloody corpses
  strown;
Yes, calmly on that dreadful scene her pale light seemed to
  shine,
As it shone on distant Bingen, – fair Bingen on the Rhine.

Alfred Noyes 1880–1958

THE ELFIN ARTIST

In a glade of an elfin forest
    When Sussex was Eden-new,
I came on an elvish painter
    And watched as his picture grew.
A harebell nodded beside him.
    He dipt his brush in its dew.

And it might be the wild thyme round him
    That shone in that dark strange ring;
But his brushes were bees' antennae,
    His knife was a wasp's blue sting;
And his gorgeous exquisite palette
    Was a butterfly's fan-shaped wing.

And he mingled its powdery colours
    And painted the lights that pass,
On a delicate cobweb canvas
    That gleamed like a magic glass,
And bloomed like a banner of elf-land
    Between two stalks of grass;

Till it shone like an angel's feather
    With sky-born opal and rose,
And gold from the foot of the rainbow,
    And colours that no man knows;
And I laughed in the sweet May weather,
    Because of the themes he chose.

For he painted the things that matter,
    The tints that we all pass by,
Like the little blue wreaths of incense
    That the wild thyme breathes to the sky;
Or the first white bud of the hawthorn,
    And the light in a blackbird's eye;

And the shadows on soft white cloud-peaks
    That carolling skylarks throw, –
Dark dots on the slumbering splendours
    That under the wild wings flow,
Wee shadows like violets trembling
    On the unseen breasts of snow;

With petals too lovely for colour
    That shake to the rapturous wings,
And grow as the bird draws near them,
    And die as he mounts and sings; –
Ah, only those exquisite brushes
    Could paint those exquisite things.

DULCE ET DECORUM EST

Bent double, like old beggars under sacks,
Knock-kneed, coughing like hags, we cursed through sludge,
Till on the haunting flares we turned our backs
And towards our distant rest began to trudge.
Men marched asleep. Many had lost their boots
But limped on, blood-shod. All went lame; all blind;
Drunk with fatigue; deaf even to the hoots
Of tired, outstripped Five-Nines that dropped behind.

Gas! GAS! Quick, boys! – An ecstasy of fumbling,
Fitting the clumsy helmets just in time;
But someone still was yelling out and stumbling,
And flound'ring like a man in fire or lime . . .
Dim, through the misty panes and thick green light,
As under a green sea, I saw him drowning.

In all my dreams, before my helpless sight,
He plunges at me, guttering, choking, drowning.

If in some smothering dreams you too could pace
Behind the wagon that we flung him in,
And watch the white eyes writhing in his face,
His hanging face, like a devil's sick of sin;
If you could hear, at every jolt, the blood
Come gargling from the froth-corrupted lungs,
Obscene as cancer, bitter as the cud
Of vile, incurable sores on innocent tongues, –
My friend, you would not tell with such high zest
To children ardent for some desperate glory,
The old Lie: Dulce et decorum est
Pro patria mori.

Thomas Love Peacock 1785–1866

THE WAR SONG OF DINAS VAWR

The mountain sheep are sweeter,
But the valley sheep are fatter;
We therefore deemed it meeter
To carry off the latter.
We made an expedition;
We met a host, and quelled it;
We forced a strong position,
And killed the men who held it.

On Dyfed's richest valley,
Where herds of kine were brousing,
We made a mighty sally,
To furnish our carousing.
Fierce warriors rushed to meet us;
We met them, and o'erthrew them:
They struggled hard to beat us;
But we conquered them, and slew them.

As we drove our prize at leisure,
The king marched forth to catch us:
His rage surpassed all measure,
But his people could not match us.
He fled to his hall-pillars;
And, ere our force we led off,
Some sacked his house and cellars,
While others cut his head off.

We there, in strife bewildering,
Spilt blood enough to swim in:
We orphaned many children,
And widowed many women.

The eagles and the ravens
We glutted with our foemen;
The heroes and the cravens,
The spearmen and the bowmen.

We brought away from battle,
And much their land bemoaned them,
Two thousand head of cattle,
And the head of him who owned them:
Ednyfed, king of Dyfed,
His head was borne before us;
His wine and beasts supplied our feasts,
And his overthrow, our chorus.

THE MILITARY HARPIST

Strangely assorted, the shape of song and the bloody man.

Under the harp's gilt shoulder and rainlike strings,
Prawn-eyed, with prawnlike bristle, well-waxed moustache,
With long tight cavalry legs, and the spurred boot
Ready upon the swell, the Old Sweat waits.

Now dies, and dies hard, the stupid, well-relished fortissimo,
Wood-wind alone inviting the liquid tone,
The voice of the holy and uncontending, the harp.

Ceasing to ruminate interracial fornications,
He raises his hands, and his wicked old mug is David's,
Pastoral, rapt, the king and the poet in innocence,
Singing Saul in himself asleep, and the ancient Devil
Clean out of countenance, as with an army of angels.

He is now where his bunion has no existence.
Breathing an atmosphere free of pipeclay and swearing,
He wears the starched nightshirt of the hereafter, his halo
Is plain manly brass with a permanent polish,
Requiring no oily rag and no Soldier's Friend.

His place is with the beloved poet of Israel,
With the wandering minnesinger and the loves of Provence,
With Blondel footsore and heartsore, the voice in the darkness
Crying like beauty bereaved beneath many a donjon,
O Richard! O King! where is the lion of England?
With Howell, Llewellyn, and far in the feral north
With the savage fame of the hero in glen and in ben,
At the morning discourse of saints in the island Eire,
And at nameless doings in the stone-circle, the dreadful grove.

Thus far into the dark do I delve for his likeness:
He harps at the Druid sacrifice, where the golden string
Sings to the golden knife and the victim's shriek.
Strangely assorted, the shape of song and the bloody man.

THE BEE MEETING

Who are these people at the bridge to meet me? They are the
  villagers –
The rector, the midwife, the sexton, the agent for bees.
In my sleeveless summery dress I have no protection,
And they are all gloved and covered, why did nobody tell me?
They are smiling and taking out veils tacked to ancient hats.

I am nude as a chicken neck, does nobody love me?
Yes, here is the secretary of bees with her white shop smock,
Buttoning the cuffs at my wrists and the slit from my neck to
  my knees.
Now I am milkweed silk, the bees will not notice.
They will not smell my fear, my fear, my fear.

Which is the rector now, is it that man in black?
Which is the midwife, is that her blue coat?
Everybody is nodding a square black head, they are knights in
  visors,
Breastplates of cheesecloth knotted under the armpits.
Their smiles and their voices are changing. I am led through a
  beanfield.

Strips of tinfoil winking like people,
Feather dusters fanning their hands in a sea of bean flowers,
Creamy bean flowers with black eyes and leaves like bored
  hearts.
Is it blood clots the tendrils are dragging up that string?
No, no, it is scarlet flowers that will one day be edible.

Now they are giving me a fashionable white straw Italian hat
And a black veil that molds to my face, they are making me
  one of them.

They are leading me to the shorn grove, the circles of hives.
Is it the hawthorn that smells so sick?
The barren body of hawthorn, etherizing its children.

Is it some operation that is taking place?
It is the surgeon my neighbors are waiting for,
This apparition in a green helmet,
Shining gloves and white suit.
Is it the butcher, the grocer, the postman, someone I know?

I cannot run, I am rooted, and the gorse hurts me
With its yellow purses, its spiky armory.
I could not run without having to run forever.
The white hive is snug as a virgin,
Sealing off her brood cells, her honey, and quietly humming.

Smoke rolls and scarves in the grove.
The mind of the hive thinks this is the end of everything.
Here they come, the outriders, on their hysterical elastics.
If I stand very still, they will think I am cow-parsley,
A gullible head untouched by their animosity,

Not even nodding, a personage in a hedgerow.
The villagers open the chambers, they are hunting the queen.
Is she hiding, is she eating honey? She is very clever.
She is old, old, old, she must live another year, and she knows
    it.
While in their fingerjoint cells the new virgins

Dream of a duel they will win inevitably,
A curtain of wax dividing them from the bride flight,
The upflight of the murderess into a heaven that loves her.
The villagers are moving the virgins, there will be no killing.
The old queen does not show herself, is she so ungrateful?

I am exhausted, I am exhausted —
Pillar of white in a blackout of knives.

I am the magician's girl who does not flinch.

The villagers are untying their disguises, they are shaking
    hands.

Whose is that long white box in the grove, what have they
    accomplished, why am I cold?

THE RAVEN

Once upon a midnight dreary, while I pondered, weak and
  weary,
Over many a quaint and curious volume of forgotten lore –
While I nodded, nearly napping, suddenly there came a tapping,
As of someone gently rapping, rapping at my chamber door.
''T is some visitor,' I muttered, 'tapping at my chamber door –
  Only this and nothing more.'

Ah, distinctly I remember it was in the bleak December;
And each separate dying ember wrought its ghost upon the
  floor.
Eagerly I wished the morrow; – vainly I had sought to borrow
From my books surcease of sorrow – sorrow for the lost
  Lenore –
For the rare and radiant maiden whom the angels name
  Lenore –
  Nameless *here* for evermore.

And the silken, sad, uncertain rustling of each purple curtain
Thrilled me – filled me with fantastic terrors never felt before;
So that now, to still the beating of my heart, I stood repeating
''T is some visitor entreating entrance at my chamber door –
Some late visitor entreating entrance at my chamber door; –
  This it is and nothing more.'

Presently my soul grew stronger; hesitating then no longer,
'Sir,' said I, 'or Madam, truly your forgiveness I implore;
But the fact is I was napping, and so gently you came rapping,
And so faintly you came tapping, tapping at my chamber door,
That I scarce was sure I heard you' – here I opened wide the
  door; –
  Darkness there and nothing more.

Deep into that darkness peering, long I stood there wondering, fearing,

Doubting, dreaming dreams no mortal ever dared to dream before;

But the silence was unbroken, and the stillness gave no token,

And the only word there spoken was the whispered word, 'Lenore!'

This I whispered, and an echo murmured back the word 'Lenore!'

Merely this and nothing more.

Back into the chamber turning, all my soul within me burning,

Soon again I heard a tapping somewhat louder than before.

'Surely,' said I, 'surely that is something at my window lattice;

Let me see, then, what thereat is, and this mystery explore –

Let my heart be still a moment and this mystery explore; –

'T is the wind and nothing more!'

Open here I flung the shutter, when, with many a flirt and flutter,

In there stepped a stately Raven of the saintly days of yore.

Not the least obeisance made he; not a minute stopped or stayed he;

But, with mien of lord or lady, perched above my chamber door –

Perched upon a bust of Pallas just above my chamber door –

Perched, and sat, and nothing more.

Then this ebony bird beguiling my sad fancy into smiling,

By the grave and stern decorum of the countenance it wore,

'Though thy crest be shorn and shaven, thou,' I said, 'art sure no craven,

Ghastly grim and ancient Raven wandering from the Nightly shore –

Tell me what thy lordly name is on the Night's Plutonian shore!'

Quoth the Raven, 'Nevermore.'

Much I marvelled this ungainly fowl to hear discourse so
    plainly,
Though its answer little meaning – little relevancy bore;
For we cannot help agreeing that no living human being
Ever yet was blessed with seeing bird above his chamber
    door –
Bird or beast upon the sculptured bust above his chamber
    door,
    With such name as 'Nevermore.'

But the Raven, sitting lonely on the placid bust, spoke only
That one word, as if his soul in that one word he did outpour.
Nothing farther then he uttered – not a feather then he
    fluttered –
Till I scarcely more than muttered 'Other friends have flown
    before –
On the morrow *he* will leave me, as my hopes have flown
    before.'
    Then the bird said 'Nevermore.'

Startled at the stillness broken by reply so aptly spoken,
'Doubtless,' said I, 'what it utters is its only stock and store
Caught from some unhappy master whom unmerciful Disaster
Followed fast and followed faster till his songs one burden
    bore –
Till the dirges of his Hope that melancholy burden bore
    Of "Never – nevermore." '

But the Raven still beguiling all my fancy into smiling,
Straight I wheeled a cushioned seat in front of bird, and bust
    and door;
Then, upon the velvet sinking, I betook myself to linking
Fancy unto fancy, thinking what this ominous bird of yore –
What this grim, ungainly, ghastly, gaunt, and ominous bird of
    yore
    Meant in croaking 'Nevermore.'

This I sat engaged in guessing, but no syllable expressing
To the fowl whose fiery eyes now burned into my bosom's
    core;
This and more I sat divining, with my head at ease reclining
On the cushion's velvet lining that the lamp-light gloated o'er,
But whose velvet violet lining with the lamp-light gloating o'er,
    She shall press, ah, nevermore!

Then, methought, the air grew denser, perfumed from an
    unseen censer
Swung by Seraphim whose foot-falls tinkled on the tufted
    floor.
'Wretch,' I cried, 'thy God hath lent thee – by these angels he
    hath sent thee
Respite – respite and nepenthe from thy memories of Lenore;
Quaff, oh quaff this kind nepenthe and forget this lost
    Lenore!'
    Quoth the Raven 'Nevermore.'

'Prophet!' said I, 'thing of evil! – prophet still, if bird or
    devil! –
Whether Tempter sent, or whether tempest tossed thee here
    ashore,
Desolate yet all undaunted, on this desert land enchanted –
On this home by Horror haunted – tell me truly, I implore –
Is there – *is* there balm in Gilead? – tell me – tell me, I
    implore!'
    Quoth the Raven 'Nevermore.'

'Prophet!' said I, 'thing of evil! – prophet still, if bird or
    devil!
By that Heaven that bends above us – by that God we both
    adore –
Tell this soul with sorrow laden if, within the distant Aidenn,
It shall clasp a sainted maiden whom the angels name Lenore –
Clasp a rare and radiant maiden whom the angels name
    Lenore.'

Quoth the Raven 'Nevermore.'

'Be that word our sign of parting, bird or fiend!' I shrieked,
    upstarting –
'Get thee back into the tempest and the Night's Plutonian
    shore!
Leave no black plume as a token of that lie thy soul hath
    spoken!
Leave my loneliness unbroken! – quit the bust above my door!
Take thy beak from out my heart, and take thy form from off
    my door!'
    Quoth the Raven 'Nevermore.'

And the Raven, never flitting, still is sitting, *still* is sitting
On the pallid bust of Pallas just above my chamber door;
And his eyes have all the seeming of a demon's that is
    dreaming,
And the lamp-light o'er him streaming throws his shadow on
    the floor;
And my soul from out that shadow that lies floating on the
    floor
    Shall be lifted – nevermore!

Alexander Pope 1688–1744

A LITTLE LEARNING

From 'An Essay On Criticism'

A little learning is a dangerous thing;
Drink deep, or taste not the Pierian spring:
There shallow draughts intoxicate the brain,
And drinking largely sobers us again.
Fired at first sight with what the Muse imparts,
In fearless youth we tempt the heights of Arts;
While from the bounded level of our mind
Short views we take, nor see the lengths behind,
But, more advanced, behold with strange surprise
New distant scenes of endless science rise!
So pleased at first the towering Alps we try,
Mount o'er the vales, and seem to tread the sky;
The eternal snows appear already past,
And the first clouds and mountains seem the last:
But those attained, we tremble to survey
The growing labours of the lengthened way;
The increasing prospect tires our wandering eyes,
Hills peep o'er hills, and Alps on Alps arise!

Peter Porter 1929–

YOUR ATTENTION PLEASE

The Polar DEW has just warned that
A nuclear rocket strike of
At least one thousand megatons
Has been launched by the enemy
Directly at our major cities.
This announcement will take
Two and a quarter minutes to make,
You therefore have a further
Eight and a quarter minutes
To comply with the shelter
Requirements published in the Civil
Defence Code – section Atomic Attack.
A specially shortened Mass
Will be broadcast at the end
Of this announcement –
Protestant and Jewish services
Will begin simultaneously –
Select your wavelength immediately
According to instructions
In the Defence Code. Do not
Take well-loved pets (including birds)
Into your shelter – they will consume
Fresh air. Leave the old and bed-
ridden, you can do nothing for them.
Remember to press the sealing
Switch when everyone is in
The shelter. Set the radiation
Aerial, turn on the geiger barometer.
Turn off your television now.
Turn off your radio immediately
The Services end. At the same time
Secure explosion plugs in the ears

Of each member of your family. Take
Down your plasma flasks. Give your children
The pills marked one and two
In the CD green container, then put
Them to bed. Do not break
The inside airlock seals until
The radiation All Clear shows
(Watch for the cuckoo in your
perspex panel), or your District
Touring Doctor rings your bell.
If before this, your air becomes
Exhausted or if any of your family
Is critically injured, administer
The capsules marked 'Valley Forge'
(Red pocket in No. 1 Survival Kit)
For painless death. (Catholics
Will have been instructed by their priests
What to do in this eventuality.)
This announcement is ending. Our President
Has already given orders for
Massive retaliation – it will be
Decisive. Some of us may die.
Remember, statistically
It is not likely to be you.
All flags are flying fully dressed
On Government buildings – the sun is shining.
Death is the least we have to fear.
We are all in the hands of God,
Whatever happens happens by His Will.
Now go quickly to your shelters.

A BIRTHDAY

My heart is like a singing bird
   Whose nest is in a watered shoot;
My heart is like an apple-tree
   Whose boughs are bent with thick-set fruit;
My heart is like a rainbow shell
   That paddles in a halcyon sea;
My heart is gladder than all these
   Because my love is come to me.

Raise me a dais of silk and down;
   Hang it with vair and purple dyes;
Carve it in doves, and pomegranates,
   And peacocks with a hundred eyes;
Work it in gold and silver grapes,
   In leaves, and silver fleurs-de-lys;
Because the birthday of my life
   Is come, my love is come to me.

Sappho – Sixth Century B.C.

HE IS MORE THAN A HERO

(Translated by Mary Barnard)

He is more than a hero

He is a god in my eyes –
the man who is allowed
to sit beside you – he

who listens intimately
to the sweet murmur of
your voice, the enticing

laughter that makes my own
heart beat fast. If I meet
you suddenly, I can't

speak – my tongue is broken;
a thin flame runs under
my skin; seeing nothing,

hearing only my own ears
drumming, I drip with sweat;
trembling shakes my body

and I turn paler than
dry grass. At such times
death isn't far from me

EVERYONE SANG

Everyone suddenly burst out singing;
And I was filled with such delight
As prisoned birds must find in freedom,
Winging wildly across the white
Orchards and dark-green fields; on – on – and out of sight.

Everyone's voice was suddenly lifted;
And beauty came like the setting sun:
My heart was shaken with tears; and horror
Drifted away . . . O, but Everyone
Was a bird; and the song was wordless; the singing will never
    be done.

JOHN OF GAUNT'S DYING SPEECH
From 'RICHARD II'

Methinks I am a prophet new inspir'd,
And thus expiring do foretell of him:
His rash fierce blaze of riot cannot last,
For violent fires soon burn out themselves;
Small showers last long, but sudden storms are short;
He tires betimes that spurs too fast betimes;
With eager feeding food doth choke the feeder:
Light vanity, insatiate cormorant,
Consuming means, soon preys upon itself.
This royal throne of kings, this scepter'd isle,
This earth of majesty, this seat of Mars,
This other Eden, demi-paradise,
This fortress built by Nature for herself
Against infection and the hand of war,
This happy breed of men, this little world,
This precious stone set in the silver sea,
Which serves it in the office of a wall,
Or as a moat defensive to a house,
Against the envy of less happier lands,
This blessed plot, this earth, this realm, this England,
This nurse, this teeming womb of royal kings,
Fear'd by their breed and famous by their birth,
Renowned for their deeds as far from home, –
For Christian service and true chivalry, –
As is the sepulchre in stubborn Jewry
Of the world's ransom, blessed Mary's Son:

This land of such dear souls, this dear, dear land,
Dear for her reputation through the world,
Is now leas'd out, – I die pronouncing it, –
Like to a tenement, or pelting farm:
England, bound in with the triumphant sea,
Whose rocky shore beats back the envious siege
Of watery Neptune, is now bound in with shame,
With inky blots, and rotten parchment bonds:
That England, that was wont to conquer others,
Hath made a shameful conquest of itself.
Ah! would the scandal vanish with my life,
How happy then were my ensuing death.

Percy Bysshe Shelley 1792–1822

TO A SKYLARK

Hail to thee, blithe Spirit!
    Bird thou never wert,
That from Heaven, or near it,
    Pourest thy full heart
In profuse strains of unpremeditated art.

Higher still and higher
    From the earth thou springest
Like a cloud of fire;
    The blue deep thou wingest,
And singing still dost soar, and soaring ever singest.

In the golden lightning
    Of the sunken sun,
O'er which clouds are bright'ning,
    Thou dost float and run;
Like an unbodied joy whose race is just begun.

The pale purple even
    Melts around thy flight;
Like a star of Heaven,
    In the broad daylight
Thou art unseen, but yet I hear thy shrill delight,

Keen as are the arrows
    Of that silver sphere,
Whose intense lamp narrows
    In the white dawn clear
Until we hardly see – we feel that it is there.

All the earth and air
    With thy voice is loud,
As, when night is bare,
    From one lonely cloud
The moon rains out her beams, and Heaven is overflowed.

What thou art we know not;
    What is most like thee?
From rainbow clouds there flow not
    Drops so bright to see
As from thy presence showers a rain of melody.

Like a Poet hidden
    In the light of thought,
Singing hymns unbidden,
    Till the world is wrought
To sympathy with hopes and fears it heeded not:

Like a high-born maiden
    In a palace-tower,
Soothing her love-laden
    Soul in secret hour
With music sweet as love, which overflows her bower:

Like a glow-worm golden
    In a dell of dew,
Scattering unbeholden
    Its aëreal hue
Among the flowers and grass, which screen it from the view!

Like a rose embowered
    In its own green leaves,
By warm winds deflowered,
    Till the scent it gives
Makes faint with too much sweet those heavy-wingèd thieves:

Sound of vernal showers
    On the twinkling grass,
Rain-awakened flowers,
    All that ever was
Joyous, and clear, and fresh, thy music doth surpass:

Teach us, Sprite or Bird,
    What sweet thoughts are thine:
I have never heard
    Praise of love or wine
That panted forth a flood of rapture so divine.

Chorus Hymeneal,
    Or triumphal chant,
Matched with thine would be all
    But an empty vaunt,
A thing wherein we feel there is some hidden want.

What objects are the fountains
    Of thy happy strain?
What fields, or waves, or mountains?
    What shapes of sky or plain?
What love of thine own kind? what ignorance of pain?

With thy clear keen joyance
    Languor cannot be:
Shadow of annoyance
    Never came near thee:
Thou lovest – but ne'er knew love's sad satiety.

Waking or asleep,
    Thou of death must deem
Things more true and deep
    Than we mortals dream,
Or how could thy notes flow in such a crystal stream?

We look before and after,
 And pine for what is not:
Our sincerest laughter
 With some pain is fraught;
Our sweetest songs are those that tell of saddest thought.

Yet if we could scorn
 Hate, and pride, and fear;
If we were things born
 Not to shed a tear,
I know not how thy joy we ever should come near.

Better than all measures
 Of delightful sound,
Better than all treasures
 That in books are found,
Thy skill to poet were, thou scorner of the ground!

Teach me half the gladness
 That thy brain must know,
Such harmonious madness
 From my lips would flow
The world should listen then – as I am listening now.

Sir Philip Sidney 1554–86

PHILOMELA

The Nightingale, as soon as April bringeth
 Unto her rested sense a perfect waking,
While late-bare Earth, proud of new clothing, springeth,
 Sings out her woes, a thorn her song-book making;
   And mournfully bewailing,
   Her throat in tunes expresseth
   What grief her breast oppresseth,
For Tereus' force on her chaste will prevailing.

 O Philomela fair, O take some gladness
 That here is juster cause of plaintful sadness!
  Thine earth now springs, mine fadeth;
 Thy thorn without, my thorn my heart invadeth.

Alas! she hath no other cause of anguish
 But Tereus' love, on her by strong hand wroken;
Wherein she suffering, all her spirits languish,
 Full womanlike complains her will was broken.
   But I, who, daily craving,
   Cannot have to content me,
   Have more cause to lament me,
Since wanting is more woe than too much having.

 O Philomela fair, O take some gladness
 That here is juster cause of plaintful sadness!
  Thine earth now springs, mine fadeth;
 Thy thorn without, my thorn my heart invadeth.

SIR BEELZEBUB

When
Sir
Beelzebub called for his syllabub in the hotel in Hell
       Where Proserpine first fell,
Blue as the gendarmerie were the waves of the sea,
       (Rocking and shocking the barmaid).

Nobody comes to give him his rum but the
Rim of the sky hippopotamus-glum
Enhances the chances to bless with a benison
Alfred Lord Tennyson crossing the bar laid
With cold vegetation from pale deputations
Of temperance workers (all signed In Memoriam)
Hoping with glory to trip up the Laureate's feet,
       (Moving in classical metres) . . .

Like Balaclava, the lava came down from the
Roof, and the sea's blue wooden gendarmerie
Took them in charge while Beelzebub roared for his rum.
      . . . None of them come!

EVOLUTION

When you were a tadpole and I was a fish,
In the Paleozoic time,
And side by side, on the ebbing tide,
We sprawled through the ooze and slime,
Or skittered with many a caudal flip
Through the depths of the Cambrian fen,
My heart was rife with the joy of life,
For I loved you even then.

Mindless we lived and mindless we loved,
And mindless at last we died;
And deep in a rift of the Caradoc drift,
We slumbered side by side.
The world turned on in the lathe of Time,
The hot lands heaved amain,
Till we caught our breath from the womb of death,
And crept into light again.

We were Amphibians, scaled and tailed,
And drab as a dead man's hand:
We coiled at ease 'neath the dripping trees,
Or trailed through the mud and sand,
Croaking and blind, with our three-clawed feet
Writing a language dumb,
With never a spark in the empty dark
To hint at a life to come.

Yet happy we lived, and happy we loved,
And happy we died once more,
Our forms were rolled in the clinging mold
Of a Neocomian shore.
The aeons came, and the aeons fled,
And the sleep that wrapped us fast

Was riven away in a newer day,
And the night of death was past.

When light and swift through the jungle trees
We swung in our airy flights;
Or breathed in the balms of the fronded palms,
In the hush of the moonless nights,
And oh! what beautiful years were these,
When our hearts clung each to each;
When life was filled, and our senses thrilled
In the first faint dawn of speech!

Thus life by life, and love by love,
We passed through the cycles strange;
And breath by breath, and death by death,
We followed the chain of change;
Till there came a time in the law of life
When over the nursing sod
The shadows broke, and the soul awoke
In a strange, dim dream of God.

God wrought our souls from the Tremadoc beds
And furnished them wings to fly;
He sowed our spawn in the world's dim dawn,
And I know that it shall not die;
Though cities have sprung above the graves
Where the crook-boned men made war,
And the ox-wain creaks o'er the buried caves
Where the mummied mammoths are.

For we know that the clod, by the grace of God,
Will quicken with voice and breath;
And we know that Love, with gentle hand,
Will beckon from death to death.
And so, as we linger at luncheon here,
O'er many a dainty dish,
Let us drink anew to the time when you
Were a tadpole and I was a fish.

TENUOUS AND PRECARIOUS

Tenuous and Precarious
Were my guardians,
Precarious and Tenuous,
Two Romans.

My father was Hazardous,
Hazardous,
Dear old man,
Three Romans.

There was my brother Spurious,
Spurious Posthumous,
Spurious was spurious
Was four Romans.

My husband was Perfidious,
He was perfidious,
Five Romans.

Surreptitious, our son,
Was surreptitious,
He was six Romans.

Our cat Tedious
Still lives,
Count not Tedious
Yet.

My name is Finis,
Finis, Finis,
I am Finis,
Six, five, four, three, two,
One Roman,
Finis.

Robert Southey 1774–1843

AFTER BLENHEIM

It was a summer evening,
    Old Kaspar's work was done,
And he before his cottage door
    Was sitting in the sun;
And by him sported on the green
His little grandchild Wilhelmine.

She saw her brother Peterkin
    Roll something large and round
Which he beside the rivulet
    In playing there had found;
He came to ask what he had found
That was so large and smooth and round.

Old Kaspar took it from the boy
    Who stood expectant by;
And then the old man shook his head,
    And with a natural sigh
''Tis some poor fellow's skull,' said he,
'Who fell in the great victory.

'I find them in the garden,
    For there's many here about,
And often when I go to plough
    The ploughshare turns them out,
For many thousand men,' said he
'Were slain in that great victory.'

'Now tell us what 'twas all about,'
    Young Peterkin he cries;
And little Wilhelmine looks up
    With wonder-waiting eyes;
'Now tell us all about the war,
And what they fought each other for.'

'It was the English,' Kaspar cried,
  'Who put the French to rout;
But what they fought each other for
  I could not well make out.
But everybody said,' quoth he,
'That 'twas a famous victory.

'My father lived at Blenheim then,
  Yon little stream hard by;
They burnt his dwelling to the ground,
  And he was forced to fly:
So with his wife and child he fled,
Nor had he where to rest his head.

'With fire and sword the country round
  Was wasted far and wide,
And many a childing mother then
  And new-born baby died:
But things like that, you know, must be
At every famous victory.

'They say it was a shocking sight
  After the field was won;
For many thousand bodies here
  Lay rotting in the sun:
But things like that, you know, must be
After a famous victory.

'Great praise the Duke of Marlbro' won
  And our good Prince Eugene;'
'Why, 'twas a very wicked thing!'
  Said little Wilhelmine;
'Nay . . . nay . . . my little girl,' quoth he,
'It was a famous victory.

'And everybody praised the Duke
  Who this great fight did win.'
'But what good came of it at last?'
  Quoth little Peterkin: –
'Why, that I cannot tell,' said he,
'But 'twas a famous victory.'

THE GOAT PATHS

The crooked paths go every way
    Upon the hill – they wind about
    Through the heather in and out
Of the quiet sunniness.
And there the goats, day after day,
    Stray in sunny quietness,
Cropping here and cropping there,
    As they pause and turn and pass,
Now a bit of heather spray,
    Now a mouthful of the grass.

In the deeper sunniness,
    In the place where nothing stirs,
Quietly in quietness,
    In the quiet of the furze,
For a time they come and lie
Staring on the roving sky.
If you approach they run away,
    They leap and stare, away they bound,
    With a sudden angry sound,

To the sunny quietude;
    Crouching down where nothing stirs
    In the silence of the furze,
Crouching down again to brood
In sunny solitude.

If I were as wise as they
    I would stray apart and brood,
I would beat a hidden way.
    Through the quiet heather spray
    To a sunny solitude;

And should you come I'd run away,
　　I would make an angry sound,
　　I would stare and turn and bound
To the deeper quietude,
　　To the place where nothing stirs
　　In the silence of the furze.

In that airy quietness
　　I would think as long as they;
Through the quiet sunniness
　　I would stray away to brood
By a hidden beaten way
　　In a sunny solitude,

I would think until I found
　　Something I can never find,
Something lying on the ground
　　In the bottom of my mind.

Robert Louis Stevenson 1850–94

THE LAMPLIGHTER

My tea is nearly ready and the sun has left the sky;
It's time to take the window to see Leerie going by;
For every night at teatime and before you take your seat,
With lantern and with ladder he comes posting up the street.

Now Tom would be a driver and Maria go to sea,
And my papa's a banker and as rich as he can be;
But I, when I am stronger and can choose what I'm to do,
O Leerie, I'll go round at night and light the lamps with you!

For we are very lucky, with a lamp before the door,
And Leerie stops to light it as he lights so many more;
And O! before you hurry by with ladder and with light,
O Leerie, see a little child and nod to him to-night!

IN THE ORCHARD

'I thought you loved me.' 'No, it was only fun.'
'When we stood there, closer than all?' 'Well, the harvest
   moon
Was shining and queer in your hair, and it turned my head.'
'That made you?' 'Yes.' 'Just the moon and the light it made
Under the tree?' 'Well, your mouth, too.' 'Yes, my mouth?'
'And the quiet there that sang like the drum in the booth.
You shouldn't have danced like that.' 'Like what?' 'So close,
With your head turned up, and the flower in your hair, a rose
That smelt all warm.' 'I loved you. I thought you knew
I wouldn't have danced like that with any but you.'
'I didn't know. I thought you knew it was fun.'
'I thought it was love you meant.' 'Well, it's done.' 'Yes, it's
   done.
I've seen boys stone a blackbird, and watched them drown
A kitten . . . it clawed at the reeds, and they pushed it down
Into the pool while it screamed. Is that fun, too?'
'Well, boys are like that . . . Your brothers . . .' 'Yes, I know.
But you, so lovely and strong! Not you! Not you!'
'They don't understand it's cruel. It's only a game.'
'And are girls fun, too?' 'No, still in a way it's the same.
It's queer and lovely to have a girl . . .' 'Go on.'
'It makes you mad for a bit to feel she's your own,
And you laugh and kiss her, and maybe you give her a ring,
But it's only in fun.' 'But I gave you everything.'
'Well, you shouldn't have done it. You know what a fellow
   thinks
When·a girl does that.' 'Yes, he talks of her over his drinks
And calls her a –' 'Stop that now. I thought you knew.'
'But it wasn't with anyone else. It was only you.'
'How did I know? I thought you wanted it too.
I thought you were like the rest. Well, what's to be done?'

'To be done?' 'Is it all right?' 'Yes.' 'Sure?' 'Yes, but why?'
'I don't know. I thought you were going to cry.
You said you had something to tell me.' 'Yes, I know.
It wasn't anything really . . . I think I'll go.'
'Yes, it's late. There's thunder about, a drop of rain
Fell on my hand in the dark. I'll see you again
At the dance next week. You're sure that everything's
    right?'
'Yes,' 'Well, I'll be going.' 'Kiss me . . .' 'Good night.' . . .
'Good night.'

Alfred, Lord Tennyson 1809–92

CROSSING THE BAR

Sunset and evening star,
  And one clear call for me!
And may there be no moaning of the bar,
  When I put out to sea,

But such a tide as moving seems asleep,
  Too full for sound and foam,
When that which drew from out the boundless deep
  Turns again home.

Twilight and evening bell,
  And after that the dark!
And may there be no sadness of farewell,
  When I embark;

For tho' from out our bourne of Time and Place
  The flood may bear me far,
I hope to see my Pilot face to face
  When I have crost the bar.

AND DEATH SHALL HAVE NO DOMINION

And death shall have no dominion.
Dead men naked they shall be one
With the man in the wind and the west moon;
When their bones are picked clean and the clean bones gone,
They shall have stars at elbow and foot;
Though they go mad they shall be sane,
Though they sink through the sea they shall rise again;
Though lovers be lost love shall not;
And death shall have no dominion.

And death shall have no dominion.
Under the windings of the sea
They lying long shall not die windily;
Twisting on racks when sinews give way,
Strapped to a wheel, yet they shall not break;
Faith in their hands shall snap in two,
And the unicorn evils run them through;
Split all ends up they shan't crack;
And death shall have no dominion.

And death shall have no dominion.
No more may gulls cry at their ears
Or waves break loud on the seashores;
Where blew a flower may a flower no more
Lift its head to the blows of the rain;
Though they be mad and dead as nails,
Heads of the characters hammer through daisies;
Break in the sun till the sun breaks down,
And death shall have no dominion.

LIGHTS OUT

I have come to the borders of sleep,
The unfathomable deep
Forest, where all must lose
Their way, however straight
Or winding, soon or late;
They can not choose.

Many a road and track
That since the dawn's first crack
Up to the forest brink
Deceived the travellers,
Suddenly now blurs,
And in they sink.

Her love ends –
Despair, ambition ends;
All pleasure and all trouble,
Although most sweet or bitter,
Here ends, in sleep that is sweeter
Than tasks most noble.

There is not any book
Or face of dearest look
That I would not turn from now
To go into the unknown
I must enter, and leave, alone,
I know not how.

The tall forest towers:
Its cloudy foliage lowers
Ahead, shelf above shelf:
Its silence I hear and obey
That I may lose my way
And myself.

R. S. Thomas 1913–

WELSH LANDSCAPE

To live in Wales is to be conscious
At dusk of the spilled blood
That went to the making of the wild sky,
Dyeing the immaculate rivers
In all their courses.
It is to be aware,
Above the noisy tractor
And hum of the machine
Of strife in the strung woods,
Vibrant with sped arrows.
You cannot live in the present,
At least not in Wales.
There is the language for instance,
The soft consonants
Strange to the ear.
There are cries in the dark at night
As owls answer the moon,
And thick ambush of shadows,
Hushed at the fields' corners
There is no present in Wales,
And no future;
There is only the past,
Brittle with relics,
Wind-bitten towers and castles
With sham ghosts;
Mouldering quarries and mines;
And an impotent people,
Sick with inbreeding,
Worrying the carcase of an old song.

AT LORD'S

It is little I repair to the matches of the Southron folk,
   Though my own red roses there may blow;
It is little I repair to the matches of the Southron folk,
   Though the red roses crest the caps, I know.
For the field is full of shades as I near the shadowy coast,
And a ghostly batsman plays to the bowling of a ghost,
And I look through my tears on a soundless-clapping host
   As the run-stealers flicker to and fro,
     To and fro: –
O my Hornby and my Barlow long ago!

James Thomson 1700–48

SPRING FLOWERS

Along the blushing borders bright with dew,
And in yon mingled wilderness of flowers,
Fair-handed Spring unbosoms every grace:
Throws out the snow-drop and the crocus first;
The daisy, primrose, violet darkly blue,
And polyanthus of unnumbered dyes;
The yellow wall-flower, stained with iron brown,
And lavish stock that scents the garden round:
From the soft wing of vernal breezes shed,
Anemonies; auriculas, enriched
With shining meal o'er all their velvet leaves;
And full ranunculas, of glowing red.
Then comes the tulip-race, where Beauty plays
Her idle freaks: from family diffused
To family, as flies the father-dust,
The varied colours run; and while they break
On the charmed eye, the exulting florist marks,
With secret pride, the wonders of his hand.
No gradual bloom is wanting; from the bud,
First-born of Spring, to Summer's musky tribes:
Nor hyacinths, deep-purpled; nor jonquils,
Of potent fragrance; nor narcissus fair,
As o'er the fabled fountain hanging still;
Nor broad carnations, nor gay-spotted pinks;
Nor, showered from every bush, the damask-rose:
Infinite numbers, delicacies, smells,
With hues on hues expression cannot paint,
The breath of Nature, and her endless bloom.

ECSTASY

I saw a frieze on whitest marble drawn
Of boys who sought for shells along the shore,
Their white feet shedding pallor in the sea,
The shallow sea, the spring-time sea of green
That faintly creamed against the cold, smooth pebbles.

The air was thin, their limbs were delicate,
The wind had graven their small eager hands
To feel the forests and the dark nights of Asia
Behind the purple bloom of the horizon,
Where sails would float and slowly melt away.

Their naked, pure, and grave, unbroken silence
Filled the soft air as gleaming, limpid water
Fills a spring sky those days where rain is lying
In shattered bright pools on the wind-dried roads,
And their sweet bodies were wind-purified.

One held a shell unto his shell-like ear
And there was music carven in his face,
His eyes half-closed, his lips just breaking open
To catch the lulling, mazy, coralline roar
Of numberless caverns filled with singing seas.

And all of them were hearkening as to singing
Of far-off voices thin and delicate,
Voices too fine for any mortal mind
To blow into the whorls of mortal ears –
And yet those sounds flowed from their grave, sweet faces.

And as I looked I heard that delicate music,
And I became as grave, as calm, as still
As those carved boys. I stood upon that shore,
I felt the cool sea dream around my feet,
My eyes were staring at the far horizon:

And the wind came and purified my limbs,
And the stars came and set within my eyes,
And snowy clouds rested upon my shoulders,
And the blue sky shimmered deep within me,
And I sang like a carven pipe of music.

PEACE

My soul, there is a country
   Far beyond the stars
Where stands a wingèd sentry
   All skilful in the wars,
There above noise and danger
   Sweet Peace sits crown'd with smiles,
And One born in a manger
   Commands the beauteous files.
He is thy gracious Friend,
   And (O my soul, awake!)
Did in pure love descend
   To die here for thy sake,
If thou canst get but thither,
   There grows the flower of Peace,
The Rose that cannot wither,
   Thy fortress, and thy ease;
Leave then thy foolish ranges;
   For none can thee secure,
But One, who never changes,
   Thy God, thy life, thy cure.

THE TIRED MAN

I am a quiet gentleman,
   And I would sit and dream;
But my wife is on the hillside,
   Wild as a hill-stream.

I am a quiet gentleman,
   And I would sit and think;
But my wife is walking the whirlwind
   Through night as black as ink.

O, give me a woman of my race
   As well controlled as I,
And let us sit by the fire,
   Patient till we die!

REQUIESCAT

Tread lightly, she is near
    Under the snow,
Speak gently, she can hear
    The daisies grow.

All her bright golden hair
    Tarnished with rust,
She that was young and fair
    Fallen to dust.

Lily-like, white as snow,
    She hardly knew
She was a woman, so
    Sweetly she grew.

Coffin board, heavy stone,
    Lie on her breast,
I vex my heart alone,
    SHE is at rest.

Peace, peace, she cannot hear
    Lyre or sonnet
All my life's buried here,
    Heap earth upon it.

THE WORLD IS TOO MUCH WITH US

The world is too much with us; late and soon,
   Getting and spending, we lay waste our powers:
   Little we see in Nature that is ours;
We have given our hearts away, a sordid boon!
This sea that bares her bosom to the moon;
   The winds that will be howling at all hours,
   And are up-gather'd now like sleeping flowers;
For this, for everything, we are out of tune;
It moves us not. – Great God! I'd rather be
   A Pagan suckled in a creed outworn;
So might I, standing on this pleasant lea,
   Have glimpses that would make me less forlorn;
Have sight of Proteus rising from the sea;
   Or hear old Triton blow his wreathèd horn.

WHEN YOU ARE OLD

When you are old and grey and full of sleep,
And nodding by the fire, take down this book,
And slowly read, and dream of the soft look
Your eyes had once, and of their shadows deep;

How many loved your moments of glad grace,
And loved your beauty with love false or true,
But one man loved the pilgrim soul in you,
And loved the sorrows of your changing face;

And bending down beside the glowing bars,
Murmur, a little sadly, how Love fled
And paced upon the mountains overhead
And hid his face amid a crowd of stars.

Benjamin Zephaniah 1958–

DIS POETRY

Dis poetry is like a riddim dat drops
De tongue fires a riddim dat shoots like shots
Dis poetry is designed fe rantin
Dance hall style, Big mouth chanting,
Dis poetry nar put yu to sleep
Preaching follow me
Like yu is blind sheep,
Dis poetry is not Party Political
Not designed fe dose who are critical.

Dis poetry is wid me when I gu to me bed
It gets into me Dreadlocks
It lingers around me head
Dis poetry goes wid me as I pedal me bike
I've tried Shakespeare, Respect due dere
But dis is de stuff I like

Dis poetry is not afraid of going ina book
Still dis poetry need ears fe hear an eyes fe hav a look
Dis poetry is Verbal Riddim, no big words involved
An if I hav a problem de riddim gets it solved,
I've tried to be more Romantic, it does nu good for me
So I tek a Reggae Riddim an build me poetry,
I could try be more personal
But you've heard it all before,
Pages of written words no needed
Brain has many words in store,
Yu could call dis poetry Dub Ranting
De tongue plays a beat
De body starts skanking,
Dis poetry is quick an childish
Dis poetry is fe de wise an foolish
Anybody can do it fe free,

Dis poetry is fe yu an me,
Don't stretch yu imagination
Dis poetry is fe de good of de Nation,
Chant,
In de morning
I chant
In de night
I chant
In de darkness
An under de spotlight,
I pass thru University
I pass thru Sociology
An den I got a Dread degree
In Dreadfull Ghettology.

Dis poetry stays wid me when I run or walk
An when I am talking to meself in poetry I talk,
Dis poetry is wid me,
Below me an above,
Dis poetry's from inside me
It goes to yu
WID LUV.

INDEX OF FIRST LINES

ACKNOWLEDGEMENTS

The publishers would like to acknowledge the following for
permission to reproduce copyright material:

Oxford University Press for 'Heidi with Blue Hair' from *The
Incident Book* by Fleur Adcock (1986); Michael Alexander for the
translation of 'From the Dream of the Rood' from *The Earliest
English Poems* (Penguin Books, 1966, 1977, 1991); Virago Press for
'And Still I Rise' by Maya Angelou; Curtis Brown Ltd, London,
for 'As I Walked Out One Evening' by W. H. Auden; Peters
Fraser & Dunlop Group Ltd for 'The Yak' by Hilaire Belloc;
Seven Springs Playground for 'Cotswold Tiles' by Edward
Berryman; Desmond Elliott on behalf of the Estate of Sir John
Betjeman for 'A Subaltern's Love Song' © John Betjeman 1979;
George J. Frimage for 'anyone lived in a pretty how town', ©
1940 by e. e. cummings, 1968 by Marion M. Cummings; Faber &
Faber Ltd for 'La Figlia Che Piange' from *Collected Poems 1909–
1962* by T. S. Eliot; Peterloo Poets for 'Not My Best Side' by U.
A. Fanthorpe from *Side Effects* (Peterloo Poets, 1978) and *Selected
Poems* (Peterloo Poets and King Penguin, 1986); Peters Fraser &
Dunlop Group Ltd for 'Song' by James Fenton; Random Century
Ltd on behalf of the Estate of Robert Frost for 'The Road Not
Taken' from *The Poetry of Robert Frost* ed. by Edward Connery
Lathem (Jonathan Cape); A. P. Watt Ltd on behalf of the
Trustees of the Robert Graves Copyright Trust for 'Flying
Crooked' from *Collected Poems 1975* by Robert Graves; Rogers,
Coleridge & White Ltd for 'Tonight at Noon' from *Collected Poems*
by Adrian Henri (Allison & Busby Ltd); Faber & Faber Ltd for 'A
March Calf' from *Season Songs* by Ted Hughes and for 'An Arundel
Tomb' from *The Whitsun Weddings* by Philip Larkin; Laurie Lee for
'April Rise'; Peggy Pykelees for 'To a Cat in a Picture Library'
from *A Traveller from Stratford and Other Poems* by Peter Leyland
(The Book Guild Press); Sheil Land Associates for 'The Miner's
Helmet' from *Collected Poems 1958–1982* by George MacBeth
(Hutchinson); David Higham Associates for 'Snow' from *Collected
Poems* by Louis MacNeice (Faber & Faber Ltd); Derek Mahon for
'A Disused Shed in Co. Wexford' from *Selected Poems* by Derek
Mahon (Viking); The Literary Trustees of Walter de la Mare and
The Society of Authors as their representative for 'The Listeners';
The Society of Authors as the literary representative of the Estate

of John Masefield for 'On Growing Old'; the Estate of the late
Edna St Vincent Millay for 'Recuerdo' from *Collected Poems* by
Edna St Vincent Millay (Harper & Row); Octopus Publishing
Group for 'King John's Christmas' from *Now We Are Six* by A. A.
Milne (Methuen Children's Books); Peters Fraser & Dunlop
Group Ltd for 'Anne Frank Huis' from *Secret Narratives* by Andrew
Motion (Salamander Press); Faber & Faber Ltd for 'The
Confirmation' from *Collected Poems* by Edwin Muir; John Murray
(Publishers) Ltd for 'The Elfin Artist' by Alfred Noyes; Random
Century Ltd for 'The Military Harpist' by Ruth Pitter (Cresset
Press); Faber & Faber Ltd for 'The Bee Meeting' from *Ariel* by
Sylvia Plath; Oxford University Press for 'Your Attention Please'
from *Peter Porter's Collected Poems* (1983); University of California
Press for 'He is More Than a Hero' from *Sappho: A New
Translation* by Mary Barnard; George T. Sassoon for 'Everyone
Sang' by Siegfried Sassoon; David Higham Associates for 'Sir
Beelzebub' from *Collected Poems* by Edith Sitwell (Macmillan);
James MacGibbon for 'Tenuous and Precarious' from *The Collected
Poems of Stevie Smith* (Penguin Twentieth Century Classics); The
Society of Authors on behalf of the copyright owner, Mrs Iris
Wise, for 'The Goat Paths' by James Stephens; Random Century
Ltd for 'In the Orchard' from *Selected Poems of Muriel Stuart*
(Jonathan Cape); David Higham Associates for 'And Death Shall
Have No Dominion' from *The Poems* by Dylan Thomas (Dent);
James and George Hepburn for 'The Tired Man' by Anna
Wickham and Benjamin Zephaniah Associates for 'Dis Poetry' ©
Benjamin Zephaniah 1984, from *City Psalms* (Bloodaxe Books).

The Publishers have made every effort to trace copyright holders
of material reproduced within this compilation. If, however, they
have inadvertently made any error they would be grateful for
notification.